UTAH STATE FARE

• A CENTENNIAL •
RECIPE COLLECTION

PAULA F. JULANDER • JOANNE R. MILNER

Library of Congress Cataloging-in-Publication Data

Julander, Paula, 1939–
    Utah state fare : a centennial recipe collection / Paula Julander and Joanne Milner.
        p.   cm.
    Includes index.
    ISBN 1-57345-082-0 (pbk.)
    1. Cookery, American. 2. Cookery—Utah. 3. Utah—Social life and customs. I. Milner, Joanne, 1957–   . II. Title.
TX715.J966   1995
641.59792—dc20   95-35785
                                                              CIP

Printed in the United States of America

10   9   8   7   6   5   4   3   2   1

CONTENTS

INTRODUCTION

Utah has unsurpassable scenery of great diversity, from 13,000-foot snow-capped mountain peaks to salt-encrusted deserts, mountain lakes and the Great Salt Lake, rugged canyon rock formations, and verdant alpine valleys. These natural beauties attract millions of visitors each year to Utah's five national parks, six national monuments, two national recreation sites, and one national historic site.

Utah also has a heritage that is rich and diverse. Ancient Native Americans roamed the land for many centuries. They were followed by Spanish and Mexican explorers and mountain men who trapped for furs. The first permanent settlers were the Mormon pioneers, who began coming to the Utah Territory in the mid-nineteenth century from the eastern states and Europe. After the Golden Spike was driven at Promontory, Utah, on May 10, 1869, marking completion of the transcontinental railroad, immigrants from Asia, Latin America, and nearly every other part of the world arrived, adding their unique customs and traditions to the state's melting pot.

On January 4, 1896, Utah became the forty-fifth state admitted to the Union. In the century since that time, the state's population has swelled, particularly in the metropolitan area between Provo and Ogden and in southwestern Utah around

St. George, and tourism has become one of the state's biggest industries. But vestiges of the state's past remain today, and many customs and traditions going back to pioneer times are still important in each of the state's nine distinctive regions.

One of those traditions centers around bounteous tables and the love of good home cooking. Many favorite recipes date to pioneer times and have been passed down through generations. Others reflect more recent culinary trends, some brought into Utah by various ethnic groups that have settled there and others brought back to the state by Utahns who have traveled worldwide.

The recipes in this book were garnered from good cooks throughout the state. Each of the sections focuses on one of the nine regions, with an introduction to the region's history, special features, and inhabitants, followed by favorite recipes, many of which are highlighted by their contributors' comments.

We hope you enjoy learning about our beautiful state and find many recipes that will be part of your own cooking repertoire for years to come. Thank you for joining with us in a celebration of Utah's centennial!

1 · BRIDGERLAND

In northeastern Utah is Bridgerland, which was originally inhabited by prehistoric hunters and gatherers some ten thousand years ago. The area was named for Jim Bridger, a famous mountain man, scout, and fur trader who explored and mapped the mountains and streams between the Bear Lake Valley and the Great Salt Lake in the mid-1820s. The area, rich in resources, was a favorite place for mountain men to rendezvous. Two of the annual Rocky Mountain trading fairs, where trappers and Indians exchanged goods at raucous gatherings each summer, took place on the shores of Bear Lake in 1826 and 1827.

In the heart of Bridgerland is Cache Valley, whose name derives from the French verb for *hide* because the early trappers concealed their pelts and supplies there. For generations it was home to Plains Indians, especially the Shoshoni, whose lifestyle centered around hunting, food gathering, and living in harmony with the cycles of nature. That culture ended after a deadly confrontation with federal troops at the battle of Bear River in 1863.

The first Anglo-Americans and Europeans to enter the region after the trappers were travelers on the Oregon Trail, along which thousands of immigrants journeyed to the Northwest during the mid-1800s. The first permanent settlers were a group of

Mormon pioneers who entered Cache Valley with a herd of cattle in 1855. When reports reached Salt Lake City that the valley had fertile soil and a favorable climate, other settlers soon followed. Remnants of the forts these early settlers built to defend themselves against Indian raids may still be seen in some of the communities they established. The Homestead Act, passed by Congress in 1862, allowed settlers to purchase land inexpensively in frontier areas, providing additional impetus to the region's growth.

Bear Lake Valley was colonized beginning in 1862 by a group led by Charles C. Rich, who was sent to the region by Brigham Young. That area became Rich County in 1868. By the late 1870s, neighboring Cache County was connected to the transcontinental railroad, which provided jobs and opened new markets for the residents. From pioneer times to the present, Cache County's prosperity has centered on farms and orchards, while Rich County, higher in elevation, has been better suited to ranching.

Dominating the slopes of the Wasatch Mountains to the east of Logan, the county seat of Cache County, is Utah State University, which was founded in 1888 as a land-grant agricultural college. Today the university is Cache County's largest employer. Each summer it hosts the Festival of the American West, which honors the traditions, folklore, and peoples of the Old West.

Bridgerland is one of the most beautiful regions in Utah, with snow-capped mountains and fertile valleys, rivers, dams, and alpine lakes. The Wellsville Mountains bordering Cache Valley on the west are believed to be the world's highest mountains to rise from such a narrow base. Logan Canyon, which winds for thirty miles through the mountains east of Logan, connects the Cache and Bear Lake valleys. Within the canyon are many campgrounds, a ski resort, hiking, cross-country skiing trails, caves, and other recreational attractions. One trail leads to the 3,200-year-old Jardine Juniper, acknowledged as the oldest juniper in the world. The canyon's eastern summit overlooks the sparkling azure-blue waters of Bear Lake, Utah's second largest freshwater lake.

The climate offers four distinct seasons, with temperatures ranging from the seventies and eighties in the summer to well below freezing in the winter; the town of Woodruff in the Bear Lake Valley holds the record for the coldest temperature ever recorded in the state, at minus-fifty degrees. Each of the seasons brings new beauty to the area, from the sparkling white of winter's snows to the myriad colors of wildflowers in mountain meadows in spring and summer, and the bright red and yellow leaves of autumn. Many animals inhabit the area as well, such as deer, elk, moose, antelope, bear, and occasional wild cats. The lakes and streams are stocked with trout and many other fish species, and Bear Lake is home to at least four species of fish found nowhere else in the world.

From the farming and dairy fields in the Cache Valley to the mountainous ranches of Bear Lake Valley, Bridgerland is a place of beauty, productivity, and historical interest. It is also a place to sample many delicious foods for which the region is well known. Cache County is the state's leading producer of dairy products; in fact, 10 percent of all hard cheese in America comes from the area, with the nation's largest Swiss cheese factory located there. Other Cache County products include honey and fruit. Raspberries grown on the hills overlooking Bear Lake attract visitors from far and near during the short growing season.

The words with which author Thomas Wolfe described Cache Valley sum up well the entire region known today as Bridgerland: "A most lovely and enchanted valley, a valley that makes all that has gone before fade as nothing."

BRIDGERLAND BARBECUED BEEF

1 beef roast (3 to 5 pounds)
Barbecue sauce
1 to 2 onions, chopped
Salt

Pepper
1½ to 2 teaspoons liquid smoke
   (optional)

Preheat oven to 325 degrees. Place the meat on a sheet of heavy-duty aluminum foil or double layer of regular-weight foil (sheet should be large enough to completely wrap around meat). Pour the sauce freely on all the surfaces of the meat. Add onions, salt, and pepper, and, if desired, liquid smoke. (Note: Slashes may be cut in the meat to facilitate faster and more uniform penetration of the sauce and other ingredients.) Bring the edges of the foil together and roll them securely so that all the juices will be trapped inside the package. Put the meat on a shallow pan, and roast in preheated oven until it reaches desired degree of doneness. This can be determined by inserting a thermometer into the center of the roast. It should register approximately 140 degrees for rare, 160 degrees for medium, or 170 degrees for well done. (A 4-pound roast will take approximately 1¾ hours for rare, 2¼ for medium, and 3 hours for well done.)

Contributor's comments: "This recipe has been a favorite for city celebrations, church socials, and company parties for many years. For a large group, roasts are often cooked for several hours in a deep pit lined with hot rocks. The meat can also be cooked over a barbecue grill."

HONEYLAND LIME MARINADE

¾ cup honey
⅓ cup vegetable oil
2 teaspoons garlic, minced

⅔ cup fresh lime juice
1 tablespoon freshly grated
   ginger root

In a mixing bowl combine honey, oil, garlic, lime juice, and grated ginger root. Mix well. May be used to marinate beef, lamb, or chicken. Makes 1¾ cups marinade.

CORNISH COUNTRY-STYLE QUAIL

6 quail, split in half
Salt
Pepper
Flour for coating quail

Oil, bacon drippings, or butter
2 tablespoons flour
1 cup water

Season each half of quail with salt and pepper to taste; coat well with flour. In a large skillet, sauté quail in hot oil, bacon drippings, or butter, until golden brown on both sides. Remove from skillet, wrap in foil, and place in a 200–degree oven while preparing gravy.

In the skillet set over medium heat, stir 2 tablespoons flour into pan drippings. Stirring constantly, add water and simmer until thickened to desired gravy consistency. Return quail to skillet, cover, and simmer until fork tender, about 20 minutes. Serves 6 (2 quail halves per serving).

BONNEVILLE CISCO

3 to 4 pounds cisco, cleaned and
    scaled
⅓ cup flour
⅓ cup cornmeal
1 teaspoon salt

½ teaspoon pepper
½ teaspoon garlic powder
Dash of tarragon
Oil for deep-fat frying

Wash fish and pat dry with paper towels. In a plastic or heavy paper bag, combine flour, cornmeal, salt, pepper, garlic powder, and tarragon. Drop fish pieces into flour mixture; coat thoroughly. Deep-fry in hot oil three minutes. *Note:* Fish may also be fried in small amount of oil in a skillet. Cook about three minutes on each side, until fish is golden brown and flakes easily. Makes 6 servings.

Contributor's comments: "Bear Lake is a valuable natural resource. The lake is at least twenty-eight thousand years old, and for eight thousand years it was isolated from the Bear River by earthquake activity. This isolation resulted in a unique water chemistry as well as rare forms of plant and animal life. Among these are four species of fish found nowhere else in the world, including Bonneville cisco and Bear Lake whitefish."

BEAR LAKE MACKINAW OR LAKE TROUT

4 to 5 pounds fish, cleaned and
    scaled
¼ cup butter or margarine
¼ teaspoon garlic powder

2 tablespoons lemon juice
1 tablespoon Parmesan cheese
Paprika
Parsley

Spread each fish open, filet-style. Cut piece of aluminum foil large enough to wrap each individual fish. Place fish, skin side down, on foil. Melt butter or margarine, and stir in garlic powder, lemon juice, and Parmesan cheese. Brush liberally over fish. Wrap with foil and bake over medium-hot coals on barbecue grill, or place on a cookie sheet and bake in oven set at 400 degrees. Bake for 10 to 15 minutes or until fish flakes easily. Do not overcook. Just before serving, lightly sprinkle with paprika and garnish with parsley. Depending on size of fish, allow one-half to one whole fish per serving.

GOLDEN CHEESE HAM BAKE

5 slices soft bread, cut in cubes
3 cups grated longhorn or cheddar
    cheese
6 eggs, slightly beaten
½ teaspoon dry mustard

2 cups milk
½ teaspoon salt
Dash of cayenne pepper
Dash of Accent
½ cup chopped ham

Place bread cubes in a 2–quart greased baking dish. Sprinkle with cheese. Combine remaining ingredients and pour over the cheese/bread mixture. Cover with foil and refrigerate 8 hours or overnight. Uncover and bake at 350 degrees for 45 minutes. Makes 4 to 6 servings.

Note: This is a favorite recipe of Jackie Leavitt, wife of Utah Governor Mike Leavitt.

CHICKEN OR TURKEY POT PIES

Pastry to cover individual pies
   (recipe below)
⅓ cup diced potatoes
⅓ cup carrot slices
⅓ cup frozen green peas
¼ cup chopped celery
½ cup boiling water
2 tablespoons butter or margarine

¼ cup flour
½ teaspoon salt
⅛ teaspoon pepper
1⅓ cups chicken or turkey broth
⅔ cup milk
1½ cups chicken or turkey, cooked
   and diced

Prepare pastry (recipe below); set aside. Boil potatoes, carrots, peas, and celery in ½ cup water until tender, about 6 minutes. Drain and set aside. In a separate saucepan over low heat, melt butter or margarine; stir in flour, salt, and pepper. Add broth and milk slowly, stirring constantly; cook until thickened. Stir in chicken or turkey and vegetables. Pour into four 1–cup baking dishes.

Top filling with pastry, folding edges of pastry over rim of dishes. Cut slits in top for steam to escape. Bake at 400 degrees for 40 minutes, or until crusts are browned and filling is bubbly. Makes 4 servings.

PASTRY FOR POT PIES

1 cup flour
¼ teaspoon salt

2 tablespoons cold water
¼ cup oil

In a large mixing bowl, combine flour and salt thoroughly. In a small bowl, mix 3 tablespoons of the flour mixture with 2 tablespoons cold water to make a paste. Set aside. Using a fork, add oil to the flour mixture in the large bowl and stir until it is crumbly. Mix in the flour paste and stir to form a ball. Divide pastry into four pieces. Roll each piece between two sheets of wax paper until it is at least 1 inch wider in diameter than the baking dishes. Set aside while preparing filling; then proceed as instructed above.

GARDEN LASAGNA

1 package (16 ounces) lasagna
    noodles
8 large carrots, sliced
1 large onion, chopped
1 clove garlic, minced
2 tablespoons olive oil
1 cup water
2 teaspoons oregano
2 teaspoons basil
2 teaspoons salt

½ teaspoon pepper
4 cans (8 ounces each) tomato sauce
3 cups fresh mushrooms, sliced
2 packages (10 ounces each) frozen
    chopped spinach
4 cups cottage cheese
3 cups grated mozzarella cheese
½ cup grated Parmesan cheese
2 eggs or 3 egg whites, lightly beaten
½ teaspoon pepper

Boil lasagna noodles as directed on package. Drain off hot water, and replace with cold water to keep noodles from sticking. Set aside. In a large pot, sauté carrots, onions, and garlic in olive oil for 5 to 7 minutes. Add water, oregano, basil, salt, ½ teaspoon pepper, and tomato sauce; cover and simmer for 15 to 20 minutes on low heat. Stir in mushrooms and simmer an additional 2 to 3 minutes. Thaw spinach and drain excess liquid. In a large mixing bowl combine cottage cheese, mozzarella cheese, Parmesan cheese, eggs, and ½ teaspoon pepper.

Grease 13 x 9–inch casserole dish. Lightly line bottom of dish with vegetable/tomato sauce; then alternate layers of noodles, sauce, spinach, and cheese mixture, ending with cheese on top. Cover dish and bake at 375 degrees for 35 minutes. Makes 12 to 15 servings.

TURKEY FRUIT SALAD

2 cups diced cooked turkey
1 medium apple, chopped
1 can (11 ounces) mandarin oranges,
    drained
1 can (8 ounces) pineapple chunks,
    drained

1 cup grapes, halved
½ cup mayonnaise
¼ teaspoon ground ginger
2 tablespoons honey
½ cup pecan halves

In a mixing bowl, combine turkey, apple, mandarin oranges, pineapple chunks, and grape halves. Set aside. In a small bowl, combine mayonnaise, ginger, and honey; mix well. Pour dressing over turkey mixture and mix lightly. Stir in pecans just before serving. Makes 6 servings.

CHEDDAR CHEESE AND VEGETABLE CHOWDER

4 cups milk
3 medium-size red potatoes, peeled
    and cut into cubes
3 medium-size carrots, sliced
1 small onion, chopped
1 teaspoon salt
1 cup fresh or frozen green peas

½ cup water
¼ cup flour
½ teaspoon dry mustard
2½ cups shredded sharp cheddar
    cheese
1 teaspoon Worcestershire sauce
¼ teaspoon pepper

In a large heavy saucepan, combine milk, potatoes, carrots, onion, and salt; bring to boil, then simmer for 10 minutes. Stir in peas, and simmer for additional 10 minutes. In a small dish, combine water, flour, and dry mustard; stir until smooth. Over medium heat, add flour mixture to soup and, stirring constantly, cook until thickened. Cook for 1 additional minute, stirring constantly. Stir in shredded cheese. Remove from heat and add Worcestershire sauce and pepper. If chowder cools before it is served, reheat it just to simmer point; do not boil. Makes 6 servings.

HEARTY CHEESE AND BROCCOLI SOUP

2 packages (10 ounces each) frozen,
    chopped broccoli, or 1½ pounds
    fresh broccoli, washed,
    trimmed, and cut in small pieces
2 tablespoons butter
4 tablespoons flour, divided

1 teaspoon marjoram
¼ teaspoon ground red pepper
4 cups milk
1½ cups shredded Swiss or cheddar
    cheese
1½ cups shredded American cheese

Cook broccoli in a small amount of water until tender. Remove from heat and set aside (do not drain). In a large heavy saucepan melt butter, then stir in 2 tablespoons of the flour, marjoram, and red pepper. Continue stirring over low heat until mixture is smooth. Add milk and, stirring constantly, heat to boiling and stir until mixture is thick and bubbly. To hot milk sauce, add broccoli and liquid in which it was cooked; heat to simmering point. Remove from heat. Toss together remaining 2 tablespoons flour and the cheeses; stir into broccoli mixture. Simmer, stirring constantly, over low heat until cheeses are melted. Makes 6 servings.

CREAMY WHIPPED POTATOES

9 baking potatoes
½ cup butter or margarine, softened
    at room temperature
1 package (8 ounces) cream cheese,
    softened at room temperature

¾ cup sour cream
½ teaspoon nutmeg
Salt and pepper to taste

Wash, peel, and dice potatoes. Boil potatoes over medium heat until tender. Drain. Place in a mixer bowl the potatoes, butter or margarine, and cream cheese. Whip with electric mixer until light and fluffy. Stir in sour cream, nutmeg, and salt and pepper to taste. Serve immediately. Makes 8 to 10 servings.

SUNDAY POTATOES

3 pounds new red potatoes
1 package (8 ounces) garlic and herb
  cream cheese, softened

2 cups whipping cream
Salt and pepper to taste

Scrub potatoes and cut in slices. (If older red potatoes are used, peel them before slicing.) In a saucepan, heat cheese and cream over medium heat until melted, stirring constantly. Stir in seasonings. Grease a 13 x 9–inch casserole dish or baking pan. Put half of the sliced potatoes in the greased dish or pan, and cover with half the cheese mixture. Add remaining potatoes, and top with remaining cheese mixture. Bake uncovered at 350 degrees for 1 hour. Makes 6 servings.

CHEESY SCALLOPED CARROTS

12 medium carrots, peeled and sliced
¼ cup butter or margarine
1 small onion, minced
¼ cup flour
1 teaspoon salt
¼ teaspoon dry mustard

2 cups milk
⅛ teaspoon pepper
¼ teaspoon celery salt
½ pound cheddar cheese
3 cups buttered bread crumbs

In a small amount of water in a saucepan, simmer or steam carrots until tender. Drain. In a separate saucepan, melt butter or margarine. Add onion and sauté for 2 to 3 minutes. Stir in flour, salt, and dry mustard. Add milk, and stir over medium heat until smooth. Add pepper and celery salt; set aside. Slice cheese. In a 2–quart buttered casserole dish, arrange a layer of carrots, then a layer of cheese slices. Repeat until both are used, ending with carrots. Pour milk sauce over carrots, and sprinkle with bread crumbs. Bake uncovered at 350 degrees for 25 minutes or until golden. Makes 8 servings.

JEAN'S SALAD

2 heads romaine lettuce
¾ cup olive oil
2 tablespoons lemon juice
3 cloves garlic, finely minced
½ teaspoon salt
½ teaspoon pepper
½ cup crisp cooked bacon, crumbled

1 cup cherry tomatoes, cut in halves
1 cup mushrooms, sliced
1 cup grated Swiss cheese
⅔ cup slivered almonds
1 cup croutons
⅓ cup Parmesan cheese

Wash lettuce and drain well. Tear into bite-size pieces, and refrigerate it until crisp. Prepare dressing by combining in a small jar the olive oil, lemon juice, minced garlic, salt, and pepper; shake well.

Place lettuce, bacon, tomatoes, mushrooms, Swiss cheese, and almonds in a large serving bowl; add dressing and toss lightly. Add croutons and Parmesan cheese just before serving. Makes 10 to 12 servings.

PARMESAN BREAD STICKS

1 package (1 tablespoon) active dry
    yeast
1½ cups warm water, divided
1 tablespoon honey
½ teaspoon salt

3 to 4 cups flour
½ cup butter or margarine
½ cup grated Parmesan cheese
Garlic salt

In a large bowl, soften yeast in ½ cup warm water. Add honey and salt. Add remaining 1 cup water to yeast mixture; stir in enough flour to make a soft dough. On floured board, roll dough out into a rectangle 1 inch thick; using a sharp knife, cut into 12 to 15 bread sticks. Place sticks about one inch apart on a greased cookie sheet. Drizzle with melted butter and sprinkle with Parmesan cheese and garlic salt. Let rise until double in size. Bake at 375 degrees for 20 to 30 minutes, depending on thickness of breadsticks. *Note:* For crisper bread sticks, roll dough out thinner. Sticks may also be twisted before letting dough rise.

SWISS CHEESE BREAD

1½ cups milk	½ cup warm water
2 teaspoons sugar or honey	5 cups white flour (approximately)
1 tablespoon salt	1 egg
2 tablespoons butter	1 tablespoon water
2 cups grated Swiss cheese	Poppy seeds
2 packages (1 tablespoon each) active dry yeast	

Scald milk. In a large bowl, combine scalded milk with sugar or honey, salt, butter, and cheese. Let cool until lukewarm. Soften yeast in ½ cup warm water, and add to milk mixture. Stir well. Gradually add flour, stirring well after each addition, until fairly stiff dough is formed. Knead dough about 5 minutes. Place dough in a greased bowl, turning once to grease top. Let rise until double in bulk. Punch dough down and divide into two equal portions. Roll each piece into an 11 x 15–inch rectangle.

Cut each rectangle lengthwise into three equal strips, leaving strips joined at one end. Braid strips loosely, and pinch ends together. Place braided loaves on a well-greased cookie sheet; cover and let rise until double in size. Beat egg with 1 tablespoon water and brush onto loaves; sprinkle with poppy seeds. Bake at 350 degrees until tops of loaves are golden brown, about 40 to 45 minutes. Makes 2 loaves.

Contributor's comments: "Cache Valley is famous for its Swiss cheese. Most of the Swiss cheese produced in the United States is made in plants east of the Mississippi. There are only two plants west of the Mississippi, and both are in Cache Valley. Swiss Cheese Bread is a favorite recipe of Delores Gossner Wheeler, president and chief executive officer of Gossner Foods in Logan."

VEGETABLE BREAD

2 packages (1 tablespoon each)
    active dry yeast
½ cup warm water
4 cups milk
¼ cup sugar
4 teaspoons salt
¼ cup butter, shortening, or oil
3 eggs, beaten
11½ to 12½ cups flour

½ cup finely chopped red cabbage
½ cup finely chopped onions
⅓ cup finely chopped celery
¼ cup finely chopped green pepper
¼ cup finely chopped cucumber,
    peeled and seeded
1 garlic clove, finely minced
¾ cup grated carrots
¼ cup alfalfa sprouts

In a small bowl, soften yeast in warm water. In a large mixing bowl, combine milk, sugar, salt, butter, eggs, and 6 cups of flour. Add yeast and mix well. Add all the vegetables and enough flour to make a soft dough. Knead well. Cover dough and let rise twice until double in bulk. Grease four 8½ x 4½ x 2½–inch loaf pans. Shape dough into 4 loaves and place in pans. Cover loaves and let rise in a warm place until double in size. Bake at 375 degrees for 35 to 40 minutes. Makes 4 loaves.

Contributor's comment: "This bread is delicious served with soups and chili, or made into sandwiches."

CACHE VALLEY CHEESECAKE

2½ pounds cream cheese, softened at
    room temperature
½ cup butter
1½ cups sugar
¼ cup cornstarch

4 large eggs
2 cups sour cream
Juice of 1 lemon
1 teaspoon vanilla
Sour Cream Topping (recipe below)

Cream together cream cheese, butter, sugar, and cornstarch. Add eggs, sour cream, lemon juice, and vanilla; mix until smooth. Line a springform pan with parchment paper; wrap outside of pan with foil. Pour batter into pan. Set springform pan in a larger pan and pour in hot water, filling halfway up the side of springform pan. Bake in oven at 450 degrees for 15 minutes; then turn oven down to 250 degrees and bake until the cake is set when tapped lightly.

Remove from oven and place on a wire rack while preparing Sour Cream Topping. After topping is spread on warm cake, return to oven and bake at 375 degrees for about 6 minutes. Remove from oven and dot with fresh raspberries. Cool at room temperature, then refrigerate until cold, at least two hours or overnight. Makes 16 servings.

SOUR CREAM TOPPING FOR CHEESECAKE

2 cups sour cream
1 teaspoon vanilla

½ cup sugar

Mix all ingredients together and spread on top of warm cake. Proceed as directed above.

DUTCH-OVEN PINEAPPLE CARROT CAKE

2 cups flour
2 teaspoons baking soda
½ teaspoon salt
2 teaspoons cinnamon
3 eggs
¾ cup salad oil
¾ cup buttermilk
2 cups sugar
2 teaspoons vanilla

1 can (8 ounces) crushed pineapple,
   drained
2 cups shredded carrots
1 cup flaked coconut
1 cup chopped nuts
Buttermilk Glaze (recipe on page 17)
Orange Cream Cheese Frosting
   (recipe on page 17)

In medium-size mixing bowl, combine flour, baking soda, salt, and cinnamon; set aside. In large mixing bowl, beat eggs. Add oil, buttermilk, sugar, and vanilla; mix well. Add flour mixture; mix well. Stir in pineapple, carrots, coconut, and nuts. Pour into a 14–inch Dutch oven. *Bake in coals for 45 minutes to 1 hour. (Use about 10 to 12 briquettes on bottom for 20 to 25 minutes, and 14 to 16 briquettes on top for the full baking time.) Test for doneness by inserting a cake tester or toothpick in center of cake; if it comes out clean and dry, cake is done. Or lightly touch center of cake with finger; if cake springs back and no imprint remains, cake is done. If cake is not quite done, bake a little longer, then test again.

Remove cake from heat and, while still hot, pour Buttermilk Glaze over cake. Cool completely, then frost with Orange Cream Cheese Frosting.

*Note: Cake may also be baked in a 13 x 9-inch greased and floured cake pan in a conventional oven. Bake at 350 degrees for 30 to 45 minutes. Test as above for doneness.

BUTTERMILK GLAZE

1 cup sugar
½ teaspoon baking soda
½ cup buttermilk

½ cup butter or margarine
1 tablespoon light corn syrup
1 teaspoon vanilla

Combine all ingredients and boil for 1 minute. Remove cake from heat when done, and while hot, pour glaze over cake. Cool completely before frosting cake.

ORANGE CREAM CHEESE FROSTING

½ cup butter or margarine, softened
1 package (8 ounces) cream cheese,
    softened
1 teaspoon vanilla

2 cups confectioners' sugar
1 teaspoon orange juice
1 teaspoon grated orange peel

Cream together butter and cream cheese. Add vanilla, confectioners' sugar, orange juice, and orange peel. Beat until thick and smooth. Frost cake and garnish with carrot curls, thin orange slice twists, or mint leaves.

Contributor's comment: "Outdoor cooking is a specialty of many Cache Valley cooks. The Dutch Oven Cook-off at the Festival of the American West, held every summer at Utah State University in Logan, attracts many outdoor cooks. This cake is a prize-winning Dutch-oven recipe."

APPLE PUDDING CAKE

1 cup sugar
¼ cup butter or margarine
1 egg
1 cup flour
1 teaspoon cinnamon
1 teaspoon baking soda
½ teaspoon salt
½ teaspoon nutmeg

½ cup chopped nuts
3 medium or 2 large apples, peeled, cored, and chopped into small pieces
Apple Pudding Cake Sauce (recipe below)
Sweetened whipped cream (optional)

Cream together sugar, butter or margarine, and egg. Stir in flour, cinnamon, baking soda, salt, and nutmeg. Add nuts and apples and mix well. Pour into a greased 8– or 9–inch square pan, and bake at 350 degrees for 35 to 45 minutes. Cool. Serve with warm Apple Pudding Cake Sauce (recipe below) and, if desired, sweetened whipped cream. Makes 8 to 10 servings.

APPLE PUDDING CAKE SAUCE

½ cup butter or margarine
½ cup evaporated milk

1 cup sugar
1 teaspoon vanilla

Combine butter or margarine, evaporated milk, and sugar in a small saucepan; simmer for 15 minutes. Do not boil. Remove from heat and add vanilla. Serve warm over Apple Pudding Cake.

FRESH FRUIT CRUMBLE

1 cup flour
¾ cup sugar
1 teaspoon baking powder
¾ teaspoon salt
1 egg
3 large apples, sliced, or
    4 or 5 peaches, sliced

¼ cup sugar
1 teaspoon cinnamon
½ cup butter or margarine, melted
½ cup chopped nuts
Sweetened whipped cream or vanilla
    ice cream

Mix flour, sugar, baking powder, salt, and egg together until crumbly. Set aside. Slice apples or peaches. Combine sugar and cinnamon, and sprinkle over fruit. Place fruit in a 9 x 11–inch baking pan. Spoon flour mixture on top of fruit. Pour melted butter over flour mixture, and sprinkle chopped nuts on top. Bake at 350 degrees for 30 minutes or until topping is golden. Serve plain or with sweetened whipped cream or ice cream. Makes 6 to 8 servings.

DANISH APPLE DESSERT

1 package (8 ounces) soda crackers,
    crushed and rolled until
    medium coarse
2 to 4 tablespoons butter

⅓ cup sugar (granulated or brown)
4 cups applesauce
Sweetened whipped cream

In a skillet over medium heat, melt butter, then add cracker crumbs and stir until brown. Remove from heat, sprinkle with sugar, and divide into fourths. In a 2-quart glass serving dish, layer applesauce and cracker crumbs, ending with crumbs. Refrigerate overnight, then top with sweetened whipped cream. Makes 6 servings.

SOURDOUGH OATMEAL COOKIES

1 cup shortening	1 teaspoon baking soda
1 cup brown sugar, firmly packed	½ teaspoon baking powder
1 cup granulated sugar	½ teaspoon salt
2 eggs	1 teaspoon cinnamon
½ cup Bridgerland Sourdough	1 teaspoon nutmeg
Starter (recipe below)	2 cups rolled oats
1 teaspoon vanilla	1 cup chopped nuts
2 cups flour	1 cup raisins

In a large mixing bowl, cream together shortening, brown sugar, granulated sugar, and eggs. Stir in sourdough starter and vanilla. Sift together flour, baking soda, baking powder, salt, cinnamon, and nutmeg; add to the sourdough mixture, and mix well. Stir in rolled oats, nuts, and raisins. Drop by rounded teaspoonfuls 2 inches apart on a greased cookie sheet. Bake at 375 degrees for 10 to 12 minutes. Makes 3 to 4 dozen cookies.

BRIDGERLAND SOURDOUGH STARTER

1 package (1 tablespoon) active dry	2 cups warm water
yeast	1 tablespoon sugar
½ cup warm water	2 cups flour

In a bowl, soften yeast in ½ cup warm water. Stir in 2 cups warm water, sugar, and flour. Beat until smooth. Cover loosely and let stand at room temperature five to ten days, stirring two or three times a day. Cover tightly and refrigerate until ready to use.

To keep starter going: After using 1 cup of starter, add ¾ cup water, ¾ cup flour, and 1 teaspoon sugar. Let stand, loosely covered, at room temperature until bubbly, at least 1 day. Refrigerate. If not used within 10 days, add 1 teaspoon sugar and repeat process every 10 days.

COX HONEY COOKIES

1½ cups shortening
2 cups sugar
2 eggs
½ cup honey
4 cups flour

½ teaspoon salt
3 teaspoons baking soda
1 teaspoon baking powder
½ cup sugar
3 teaspoons cinnamon

In a large mixing bowl, cream shortening, 2 cups sugar, eggs, and honey. Sift together flour, salt, baking soda, and baking powder. Stir into creamed mixture. Combine ½ cup sugar and 3 teaspoons cinnamon. Form heaping teaspoonfuls of dough into balls, and roll each ball in sugar/cinnamon mixture. Place balls on a greased cookie sheet. Bake at 325 degrees for 8 to 10 minutes, or until lightly browned. Do not overbake. Makes 3 dozen cookies.

DANISH SWEET DESSERT SOUP

4 cups canned or bottled plums,
    including juice
½ cup golden raisins
½ cup currants
½ cup prunes, pitted and chopped

½ cup sugar
3 tablespoons quick-cooking tapioca
2 or 3 lemon slices
Small cinnamon stick
Sweetened whipped cream

In a large saucepan, combine plums and juice, raisins, currants, prunes, and sugar. Simmer for 10 minutes. Add tapioca, lemon slices, and cinnamon stick. Continue cooking over low heat, stirring constantly, until tapioca is clear and pudding starts to thicken. Spoon into dishes. Serve either hot or cold with cream or sweetened whipped cream. Makes 6 servings.

Contributor's comment: "Other fruits and juices may be substituted for plums, for variation. I frequently use apricots or peaches."

BEAR LAKE RASPBERRY PIE

1 cup sugar
2 cups water
2 tablespoons cornstarch
¼ cup cold water
2 packages (3 ounces each)
    raspberry gelatin

6 to 7 cups fresh or frozen
    raspberries, mashed
1 9-inch baked pie shell
Sweetened whipped cream

In a heavy saucepan, bring sugar and 2 cups water to a boil. In a cup, combine cornstarch and ¼ cup cold water; stir to dissolve. Add cornstarch to boiling mixture, and stir over medium heat until mixture becomes thick and clear. Add gelatin to mixture and stir until dissolved. Remove from heat, and cool to room temperature. Add raspberries. Pour into prepared pie shell; chill. Serve with sweetened whipped cream. Makes 6 to 8 servings.

FROZEN RASPBERRY DESSERT

½ cup butter or margarine
1 cup flour
¼ cup brown sugar
1 cup pecans or walnuts, chopped
2 egg whites

1 cup granulated sugar
1 package (10 ounces) frozen
    raspberries, thawed
1 cup whipping cream

In a medium-size bowl, combine butter or margarine, flour, brown sugar, and chopped nuts to make a crumb mixture. Spread mixture on a cookie sheet and bake at 350 degrees for 15 minutes, stirring every 5 minutes. Cool. Sprinkle half of crumb mixture in the bottom of a 13 x 9–inch glass dish. In a separate large mixing bowl, combine egg whites, granulated sugar, and thawed raspberries (including juice). Beat together at high speed for 15 to 20 minutes. In a separate bowl, beat whipping cream. Fold whipped cream into raspberry mixture. Pour on top of crumb mixture. Sprinkle top with remaining crumb mixture. Freeze before serving. Makes 10 to 12 servings.

RASPBERRY SAUCE

2 cups fresh raspberries
⅓ cup light corn syrup

1 tablespoon cornstarch
1½ tablespoons water

Wash and drain raspberries, then puree by pressing through a fine sieve or food mill to strain out the seeds. Combine raspberry puree and corn syrup in a saucepan. Dissolve cornstarch in water and add to the berry mixture. Cover and simmer over low heat until sauce begins to boil and thickens. Serve hot or cold over pancakes, waffles, or ice cream. Makes approximately 1½ cups sauce.

Note: Frozen raspberries may be used if fresh ones are not available. Defrost before preparing sauce.

RASPBERRY JELLY

3 cups fresh raspberries

1½ cups sugar

Wash two 8-ounce glass jelly containers in very hot water. Cover with a clean dish towel and set aside. Wash and drain raspberries; then puree by pressing through a fine sieve or food mill to strain out the seeds. Set aside. Place sugar in a cake or other small baking pan and heat in a 200–degree oven. While sugar is heating, heat puree in a saucepan until it comes to a boil; skim off foam and remove from heat. Add warm sugar and stir constantly for 10 minutes (don't whip), until sugar is well dissolved. Put jelly into sterilized glass containers and seal with paraffin wax. Cover with lid. Makes 2 cups jelly.

GARDEN CITY RASPBERRY FRAPPÉ

1½ cups sugar
3 cups water
1 can (16 ounces) frozen orange
    juice, undiluted

1 can (8 ounces) crushed pineapple,
    undrained
2½ cups fresh raspberries
Ginger ale

In a large saucepan, combine sugar and water; boil until sugar is dissolved. Cool; then add orange juice concentrate, undrained pineapple, and raspberries. Freeze until consistency of slush. Add ginger ale to taste. Makes 16 to 20 servings, about 4 ounces each.

Contributor's comments: "Garden City, on the shores of Bear Lake, is noted for its delicious raspberries. From the time the city was first established, most of the settlers here had apple trees and two or three rows of raspberry bushes in their backyards. Raspberries were not grown for large-scale commercial sale until 1938, when LaVoy Hildt decided to see if there was a market for the high-quality berries he was raising on the hills rising from the western shore of the lake. He started out by planting ten acres. Some of his neighbors thought he was crazy, but he knew what he was doing. His business prospered and continued to grow every year as the Bear Lake raspberry gained a national reputation. Today members of the Hildt family still grow all of the Bear Lake raspberries sold commercially."

CACHE COUNTY PENOCHE

6 cups sugar
½ cup warm water

2 cups whipping cream
⅓ cup light corn syrup

In a heavy saucepan or frying pan, melt 1 cup of the sugar over medium heat until the granules liquefy and become caramel in color. In another heavy saucepan, bring ½ cup water to a boil over medium heat. Slowly pour caramelized sugar into water, stirring constantly. Add remaining 5 cups sugar, cream, and corn syrup. Stir well. Stirring constantly, heat to a soft-ball stage, approximately 240 degrees F. when tested with a candy thermometer, or until a little mixture, dropped in cold water, can be formed into a soft ball. Pour on an unbuttered marble slab; cool. Beat with a wooden spatula until candy mixture is creamy. Spread candy on a buttered cookie sheet. Cool, then cut in squares. Makes 3 pounds candy.

SOFT NUTTY CARAMELS

2 cups sugar
1⅓ cups light corn syrup
3 cups heavy whipping cream

2 teaspoons vanilla
¼ teaspoon salt
1 cup chopped walnuts

In a heavy saucepan, combine sugar, corn syrup, and 1 cup of the whipping cream. Stirring constantly, cook over medium heat until mixture reaches 230 degrees as registered on a candy thermometer. Add second cup of cream, and heat to 230 degrees again. Add final cup of cream, and stir constantly until mixture reaches soft-ball stage, about 240 degrees. Remove from heat and stir in vanilla, salt, and nuts. Pour quickly onto a marble slab or a buttered cookie sheet. Cool. Cut into individual pieces and wrap in wax paper. Makes 1½ pounds candy.

Contributor's comments: "It might be said that Cache Valley residents have a sweet tooth, as evidenced by the excellent commercial candy companies in the area. Many Cache Valley families also have a rich candy-making tradition. But a word of warning: these are not quick and easy candy recipes. It takes time and elbow grease to make the Penuche and Caramels, but it is well worth the effort. Try these favorite recipes and judge for yourself."

Melon Mint Cocktail (p. 41); Pioneer Soda Bread (p. 102); Panguitch Potato Casserole (p. 76); Sanpete Carrots (p. 189); Country-Style Lamb (p. 185).

Top to bottom: Chocolate Potato Cake (p. 126) with Lemon Sauce (p. 83); Castle Valley Jelly Roll (p. 67); Mom's Apple Dumplings (p. 198).

2 · CANYONLANDS

Canyonlands, in the southeastern corner of Utah, is home to two national parks, three national monuments, several state parks, and rock formations unlike any others in the world. The natural beauty of the region, marked by towering natural bridges, spires, pinnacles, and deep canyons, has long attracted photographers and filmmakers, providing the backdrop for many movies, commercials, and advertising layouts.

Canyonlands National Park, the largest of the national parks in the region, is carved by the Colorado River and the Green River, which converge inside the canyon. The northern end of the canyon can be viewed from Dead Horse Point State Park, two thousand feet above the river and one of the most photographed spots in Utah. Cowboys at one time used this area as a natural corral for wild horses; when a large group of the animals were abandoned and died of thirst, the place came to be known as Dead Horse Point.

Arches National Park boasts the world's largest concentration of sandstone arches, with more than seven hundred within the park's boundary. Landscape Arch, the longest natural span in the world, while only a few feet in thickness, is 291 feet long and 118 feet high.

Glen Canyon National Recreation Area, which was carved by the Colorado River, empties into Lake Powell, the second largest man-made lake in America, with nearly two thousand miles of jagged canyon shoreline. The lake was named for John Wesley Powell, the first white man to navigate the Colorado River, and is Utah's number-two tourist attraction (second only to Temple Square in Salt Lake City). It is also the only place in the world where striped bass swim in abundance.

Rainbow Bridge, the world's largest natural bridge, is accessible only by boat on Lake Powell or by foot or horseback over rugged mountains and lava beds. Considered a sacred site by the Navajo Indians, the bridge is on the Navajo Indian Reservation, which covers 25,000 square miles in Utah, Arizona, and New Mexico.

The earliest known inhabitants in Canyonlands were hunter-gatherers who roamed the area 12,000 years ago in search of edible plants and game. They did not build homes, but evidences of their life-style have been found in several natural caves. From A.D. 300 to A.D. 1300, the Anasazi developed a relatively advanced civilization; many ruins and petroglyphs bear record of their culture. Spanish expeditions in the late 1700s and early 1800s found bands of Ute Indians, who were also nomadic hunter-gatherers.

In 1855 Mormon Church president Brigham Young sent a group to Elk Mountain (later renamed Moab) to build a fort to control the crossing of the Colorado River on the Old Spanish Trail. Because of hostilities with the Utes, they abandoned the fort within three years. It was not until after 1870 that permanent settlements began to be established in Canyonlands, with agriculture and mining as the main industries. Today much of the region's economy is driven by tourism, as tens of thousands each year take advantage of the wide range of outdoor activities in one of Utah's most scenic regions.

Today Canyonlands is rich in Indian tradition, from the modern Navajo to the ancient Pueblo. North of the Four Corners, the only spot in America where one can stand in four states (Utah, Colorado, New Mexico, and Arizona) at once, is Hovenweep National Monument, where clusters of ancient Pueblo ruins still stand. There, more than three hundred years before Christopher Columbus arrived in the New World, the Pueblos cultivated corn, beans, and squash and built multistoried towers, houses, kivas, storage shelters, and dams. Nearby, Newspaper Rock contains over 350 petroglyphs spanning a thousand years and covering three distinct periods.

In addition to the natural beauties of Canyonlands, the region has a rich heritage in its foods. Native American and Spanish influences can be seen in such traditional foods as Navajo fry bread, enchiladas, and chili rellenos. Ranching and the region's cowboy culture have had a major impact on the region's cuisine as well as its economy, contributing such dishes as shepherd's pie, barbecue beef, and Dutch-oven potatoes. Nuts and fruits grown locally are also popular with Canyonlands cooks. Black walnuts from trees in the Moab area are important ingredients for delicious cakes, brownies, and candies, while the bountiful peaches, cherries, melons, and other fruits are found in pies, cakes, and salsas.

SHEPHERD'S PIE

1 cup carrot slices
1½ pounds lean ground beef
1 cup chopped onion
1 cup canned green beans
1 cup canned tomatoes, diced
1 cup sliced mushrooms
1½ teaspoons Worcestershire sauce
2½ tablespoons flour

1 cup beef broth
5 medium potatoes, peeled and
     cubed
¼ cup butter or margarine
½ cup milk, heated
¼ cup chopped parsley
Salt and pepper to taste

In a small saucepan, steam carrot slices; remove from heat and set aside. In a heavy skillet over medium heat, brown ground beef and onion. Drain excess fat. Stir in steamed carrots, green beans, tomatoes, mushrooms, and Worcestershire sauce; simmer for about 10 minutes. In a small bowl, blend flour and beef broth until smooth. Stir into meat mixture, and simmer 5 minutes. Pour into a 2-quart casserole dish. Set aside. Boil potatoes until tender. Mash with butter or margarine and milk; then stir in parsley and salt and pepper. Spread mashed potatoes over meat. Bake uncovered at 350 degrees for 20 minutes, or until potatoes are golden brown. Makes 6 to 8 servings.

HAMBURGER HASH

1 pound lean ground beef
1 tablespoon cooking oil
1 large onion, chopped
1 green pepper, chopped
2 cups canned tomatoes, diced or
     chopped

½ cup uncooked rice
1 teaspoon salt
⅛ teaspoon pepper
1½ teaspoons chili powder

In a large skillet, brown beef in oil. Add onions and green pepper, and sauté until vegetables are tender. Drain off excess fat. Stir in tomatoes with juice, rice, salt, pepper, and chili powder. Pour into a 2-quart casserole dish; cover and bake at 350 degrees for 1 hour. Makes 6 servings.

MOAB MEAT LOAF

1½ pounds ground beef
3 slices bread, crumbled
½ cup milk
2 eggs, beaten
¼ cup chopped onion
¼ cup chopped green pepper
2 tablespoons chopped celery

1 teaspoon salt
⅛ teaspoon pepper
½ teaspoon dry mustard
¾ teaspoon dried sage
1 teaspoon Worcestershire sauce
¼ cup chili sauce
½ cup catsup

In a large bowl, combine ground beef, crumbled bread, milk, and beaten eggs. Add onion, green pepper, celery, salt, pepper, dry mustard, sage, Worcestershire sauce, and chili sauce. Form into a loaf and put into an ungreased loaf pan. Make slashes on top of meat loaf, and fill with catsup. Cover with aluminum foil. Bake at 350 degrees for 30 minutes; then remove foil and bake for an additional 30 minutes. Makes 8 servings.

BARBECUE BEEF

3 pounds lean ground beef
1 medium green pepper, chopped
    fine
3 medium onions, chopped fine
3 cups catsup
1 can (8 ounces) tomato sauce
2 tablespoons Worcestershire sauce

1 teaspoon dry mustard
1 teaspoon pepper
2 teaspoons salt
1 tablespoon vinegar
2 tablespoons brown sugar
2 tablespoons granulated sugar

In a large skillet, brown ground beef. Add green pepper and onion, and sauté until vegetables are tender. Drain excess fat. Add catsup, tomato sauce, Worcestershire sauce, mustard, pepper, salt, vinegar, and sugars. Simmer over low heat till thick, about 45 minutes. Serve over pasta or rice, or on sandwich buns. Makes 15 to 20 servings.

DAD'S DUTCH-OVEN POTATOES

1 pound bacon, cut into small pieces
2 to 3 cups chopped onion

10 pounds potatoes, peeled and
   sliced
Salt and pepper to taste

Heat a 14-inch Dutch oven over fire. Remove and add bacon. Cook, stirring often, at edge of fire till bacon is almost done. Drain off at least half the grease. Add onion, and cook until tender. Add potatoes, salt, and pepper. Cover and cook, stirring every 10 minutes, until done. Makes 12 to 15 servings.

Contributor's comments: "No picnic on the mountain or Boy Scout dinner in our area is complete without these potatoes. My children always request them when they come to visit us."

PORK CHILI VERDE

1½ pounds pork, cubed
3 tablespoons flour
2 tablespoons oil
1 garlic clove, minced
1 can (8 ounces) green chilies,
   chopped

2 cups water
1 cup canned tomatoes, chopped or
   diced, with juice
Salt to taste
6 to 8 flour tortillas (see index for
   recipe)

Dredge pork in flour; coat evenly. In a heavy skillet, brown pork in hot oil for about 10 minutes. Reduce heat and add garlic, green chilies, water, tomatoes, and salt. Mix well. Cover pan and simmer for at least 45 minutes, stirring occasionally so it won't stick or burn on the bottom. Serve with flour tortillas. Makes 6 to 8 servings.

POTATO AND CORN CHOWDER

1 cup chopped onion
1 cup diced celery
2½ cups peeled and diced potatoes
1 can (11 ounces) chicken broth
1½ cups water
¼ cup butter or margarine

6 tablespoons flour
2 cups milk
2 cups diced ham
1 can (16 ounces) whole kernel corn
Salt and pepper to taste

In a heavy saucepan, combine onion, celery, potatoes, chicken broth, and water. Bring to a boil, then reduce heat and simmer until vegetables are tender. In a separate heavy saucepan, melt butter or margarine over medium heat; add flour and stir until bubbly. Add milk and stir until smooth. Then add vegetable and broth mixture, ham, corn, and salt and pepper. Simmer for 2 to 3 minutes. Makes 6 servings.

SAN JUAN CHIMICHANGAS

2½ pounds beef roast, cooked and
    shredded
1 onion, chopped
2 tablespoons oil
2 tablespoons flour
1 can (8 ounces) green chilies,
    chopped

1 can (16 ounces) green chili salsa
Dash of garlic powder
Dash of cumin
2 teaspoons salt
12 large flour tortillas (see index for
    recipe)
Oil for deep-frying

In a heavy skillet, brown beef and onions in oil. Sprinkle flour over meat mixture and stir to blend. Add chilies, salsa, garlic powder, cumin, and salt; simmer for 10 minutes. Cool meat mixture, then roll in flour tortillas. Deep-fry until brown. Serve with favorite toppings, such as green chili salsa, tomatoes, sour cream, olives, lettuce, guacamole. Makes 12 servings.

CHICKEN ENCHILADAS

12 corn tortillas (see index for
   recipe)
Cooking oil, heated
1½ cups chopped cooked chicken
1 large onion, chopped
¼ cup butter or margarine
¼ cup flour

2 cups chicken broth
1 cup sour cream
1 can (8 ounces) green chilies,
   chopped
1½ cups grated cheddar or
   longhorn cheese

Dip corn tortillas one at a time in hot oil until flexible, about 5 seconds. Fill tortillas with chopped chicken and onion. Roll and place in a single layer in a 13 x 9–inch baking dish. In a heavy saucepan, melt butter or margarine over medium heat. Add flour and stir until mixture bubbles. Add chicken broth and stir constantly until mixture thickens. Remove from heat. Add sour cream and green chilies. Stir. Pour over chicken-filled tortillas. Top with grated cheese. Cover and bake at 350 degrees for 30 minutes. Makes 6 to 8 servings.

CHILI RELLENO BAKE

1 cup half-and-half
2 eggs
⅓ cup flour
2 cans (8 ounces each) whole green
   chilies

½ cup grated jack cheese
½ cup grated longhorn cheese
1 can (8 ounces) tomato sauce
Dash garlic powder
Dash cumin

In a mixing bowl, combine half-and-half with eggs and flour. Set aside. Rinse and split chilies. In a separate bowl, toss cheeses together, reserving ½ cup for top. In a 2–quart buttered casserole dish, alternately layer chilies, cheese, and milk mixture. Mix tomato sauce, garlic powder, and cumin; pour over casserole. Sprinkle with ½ cup cheese. Bake uncovered at 350 degrees for 40 minutes. Makes 4 to 6 servings.

ALICE'S NAVAJO FRY BREAD

4 cups flour
2 teaspoons baking powder
1 teaspoon salt

2 cups warm water
Lard or shortening for deep-frying

In a large bowl, combine flour, baking powder, and salt. Add water in small amounts, mixing between each addition. Knead dough till soft but not sticky. Cover and let stand 15 minutes. Pull off egg-sized balls and roll each into a round about ¼ inch thick. Prick with fork 3 or 4 times to allow dough to puff up when it is fried. Deep-fry in hot fat in heavy skillet. Fry bread may be used to prepare Navajo Tacos (below). It is also good served with mutton stew, spread with jam, or sprinkled with powdered sugar or salt. Makes 16 to 20 rounds.

NAVAJO TACOS

Alice's Navajo Fry Bread (recipe above)
6 cups canned chili beans

Shredded lettuce
Chopped tomatoes
Shredded cheese

Top each round of fry bread with ½ to 1 cup chili beans. Garnish with lettuce, tomatoes, and cheese.

CORN TORTILLAS

1 egg
1½ cups milk
1 cup flour

1 teaspoon salt
1 cup cornmeal
2 tablespoons butter, melted

In a mixing bowl, beat egg, then stir in milk. Add flour, salt, cornmeal, and butter. Mix with an egg beater or wire whip until smooth. Heat griddle until drops of cold water dance on the surface; then lightly grease it. Pour out ¼ cup of batter for each tortilla and spread into a thin circle. Cook until lightly browned on each side. Makes 20 tortillas.

FLOUR TORTILLAS

2 cups flour
½ teaspoon salt
1 teaspoon baking powder

3 tablespoons shortening
⅓ cup water

In a bowl, combine flour, salt, and baking powder. With two knives, cut shortening into flour mixture until mixture is as coarse as peas. With a fork, add just enough water to make a soft dough. Divide into 8 balls. Let rest on a floured board 10 minutes. Roll each ball into a flat round about ⅛–inch thick. Cook rounds on a hot, ungreased griddle until lightly browned but still pliable. Makes 8 tortillas.

MONTICELLO SOPAIPILLAS

1 package (1 tablespoon) active dry
    yeast
3 cups warm water
6 tablespoons shortening
2 tablespoons sugar

2 teaspoons salt
6 tablespoons nonfat dry milk
6½ cups flour
Fat for frying

In a large bowl, dissolve yeast in warm water. Add shortening, sugar, salt, and dry milk. Stir in flour to make a soft dough. Mix well. Knead dough 15 to 20 times; set aside to rest for 10 minutes. Roll dough to ¼-inch in thickness; cut in squares or triangles. Fry, turning once, in hot fat until lightly browned on each side. Makes 20 to 24 sopaipillas.

CORN BREAD

2 cups flour
2 cups yellow cornmeal
½ cup sugar
2½ teaspoons baking powder

1½ teaspoons salt
4 eggs
2 cups milk
½ cup margarine, melted

In a mixing bowl combine flour, cornmeal, sugar, baking powder, and salt. Add eggs, milk, and margarine. Beat just to blend. Pour into a buttered 9 x 13–inch baking pan. Bake at 425 degrees for 25 to 30 minutes. Makes 12 servings.

BERDENE'S HOMEMADE BREAD

4½ cups lukewarm water
3 tablespoons sugar
2 packages (1 tablespoon each)
   active dry yeast

9½ to 10 cups flour
½ cup plus 2 tablespoons shortening
1 tablespoon salt

In a large mixing bowl, combine lukewarm water, sugar, and yeast. Let yeast rise to surface. Add 5 cups of the flour, shortening, and salt. Mix well. Add about 4½ to 5 cups more flour to make a soft dough. Knead well. Cover with a clean dishtowel and let rise till double in bulk, then knead. Cover and let rise again till almost double. Knead again. Form into loaves, and put in greased bread tins. Cover and let rise in a warm place 25 to 30 minutes. Bake at 400 degrees for 35 to 40 minutes. Brush tops with butter or margarine while hot. Makes 4 loaves.

Contributor's comments: "This is my sister Berdene's prize-winning and economical bread recipe. All our family and many friends use it. It's delicious!"

DUTCH BABY PANCAKE

⅓ cup butter or margarine
4 eggs
1 cup milk

1 cup flour
Nutmeg

In an ovenproof heavy skillet or pan, melt butter or margarine. Set aside. In a bowl, blend eggs, milk, and flour. Pour into skillet over melted butter. Bake at 425 degrees for 25 minutes, or until puffy and well browned. Remove from oven and sprinkle with nutmeg. Serve at once with maple syrup, ham or bacon, or fresh fruit (sliced peaches or strawberries are especially good) and sweetened whipped cream. Makes 4 to 6 servings.

MELON SALSA

½ cup white vinegar
½ cup sugar
½ cup currants
⅓ cup sliced green onions
1 garlic clove, chopped
½ teaspoon dried cilantro

⅛ teaspoon red pepper flakes
3 cups diced cantaloupe
1 jalapeño pepper, seeded and finely
    diced
¼ cup lime juice

Combine vinegar and sugar in a small saucepan; bring to a boil, stirring until sugar dissolves. Stir in currants, green onions, garlic, cilantro, and red pepper flakes; cook 3 minutes. Add cantaloupe, jalapeño pepper, and lime juice. Bring mixture to boil; remove from heat. Put into hot sterilized jars and seal, or allow to cool and serve. Makes 2 pints.

MELON MINT COCKTAIL

2 cups sugar
1 cup water
¼ cup lemon juice

6 to 8 sprigs fresh mint
2 cups cantaloupe balls
2 cups honeydew balls

In a saucepan, bring sugar and water to a boil. Remove from heat, and add lemon juice and fresh mint. Chill. Pour mixture over combined melon balls. Chill for a few hours. Remove mint leaves before serving. Makes 6 to 8 servings.

BLACK-WALNUT AND COCONUT CAKE

½ cup butter
½ cup shortening
2 cups sugar
5 eggs, separated
1 cup buttermilk
1 teaspoon baking soda
2 cups flour

1 teaspoon vanilla
1½ cups black walnuts, chopped
3 ounces coconut, flaked
½ teaspoon cream of tartar
Cream Cheese Frosting (recipe
  below)

In a large mixing bowl, cream butter and shortening. Gradually add sugar, beating until light and fluffy and sugar is dissolved. Add egg yolks and beat well. In a separate bowl, combine baking soda and buttermilk. Stir until soda is dissolved. Add flour to creamed mixture alternately with buttermilk mixture, beginning and ending with flour. Add vanilla, black walnuts, and coconut. Mix well. Beat egg whites with cream of tartar until stiff peaks form, then fold into batter. Pour batter into 3 greased and floured 9–inch cake pans, and bake at 350 degrees for 30 minutes or until a toothpick inserted in the center comes out clean. Cool 10 minutes before removing from pans. Frost with Cream Cheese Frosting and sprinkle top of cake with black walnuts.

CREAM CHEESE FROSTING

1 package (8 ounces) cream cheese,
  softened

4½ cups confectioners' sugar
1½ teaspoons vanilla

In a large bowl, beat the cream cheese until smooth. Gradually beat in confectioners' sugar and vanilla. Beat until frosting is of spreading consistency, adding a little evaporated milk or cream, if necessary.

BLACK-WALNUT COCOA CAKE

2 cups flour
2 cups sugar
1 teaspoon baking soda
½ teaspoon salt
1 cup butter or margarine

¼ cup cocoa
1 cup water
½ cup buttermilk
2 eggs
Black-Walnut Icing (recipe below)

In a large mixing bowl, combine flour, sugar, baking soda, and salt. Set aside. In a saucepan, melt butter or margarine. Stir in cocoa and water. Bring mixture to a rapid boil; then pour over dry ingredients. Stir in buttermilk and eggs; mix well. Pour batter into a greased 15½ x 10½ x 1–inch jelly-roll pan. Bake at 350 degrees for 15 to 20 minutes, or until cake springs back when touched lightly; do not overbake. Remove from oven and allow to cool. Then spread with hot Black-Walnut Icing.

BLACK-WALNUT ICING

½ cup butter or margarine
¼ cup cocoa
½ cup buttermilk

4½ cups (1 pound) confectioners'
sugar
1 cup black walnuts, chopped

In a saucepan, melt butter or margarine. Add cocoa and buttermilk. Bring to a boil. Remove from heat and stir in confectioners' sugar and black walnuts. Spread on cake while icing is still hot.

BLACK-WALNUT BROWNIES

1¼ cups butter or margarine, melted
¾ cup cocoa
2 cups sugar
4 eggs
1 tablespoon vanilla

1¼ cups flour
½ teaspoon salt
⅛ teaspoon baking powder
1 cup black walnuts, chopped

In a large mixing bowl, combine butter or margarine, cocoa, sugar, eggs, and vanilla; blend well. In a separate bowl, sift together flour, salt, and baking powder. Add to cocoa mixture and stir until smooth. Add nuts. Pour batter into a greased and floured 15½ x 10½ x 1–inch jelly-roll pan, and spread evenly. Bake at 350 degrees for 25 minutes. Cool before cutting into bars.

BAKED CUSTARD

3 cups milk
3 eggs, well beaten
⅓ cup sugar

¼ teaspoon salt
1 teaspoon vanilla
⅛ teaspoon nutmeg

In a heavy saucepan over medium heat, scald milk. Remove from heat and cool to room temperature. When cool, add eggs, sugar, salt, vanilla, and nutmeg. Stir well. Pour into a buttered 1–quart baking dish. Place baking dish in a pan of hot water. Bake at 350 degrees for 30 to 40 minutes. The custard is done when knife inserted in center comes out clean. Makes 6 servings.

MARY'S CHERRY PIE

Pastry for 1 two-crust pie
3 cups frozen pie cherries
1½ cups sugar
¼ cup cornstarch
¼ teaspoon almond extract

Red food coloring (optional)
2 tablespoons butter
Milk
Sugar

Prepare pastry for two-crust pie, using your favorite recipe. Line a 9–inch pie plate with bottom pastry crust; roll out top crust. In a heavy saucepan, combine cherries, sugar, and cornstarch. Simmer over medium heat until cherry mixture thickens. Remove from heat and add almond extract and, if desired, red food coloring. Pour into lined pie plate, and dot with butter. Adjust top crust over filling, trimming excess pastry. Make several slits in top crust so steam can escape; then brush lightly with milk and sprinkle with sugar. Bake at 400 degrees for 45 minutes or until crust is golden brown. Serves 6 to 8.

OLD-FASHIONED APPLE PIE

Pastry for 1 two-crust pie
4 cups peeled and sliced cooking
    apples
1 cup sugar
¼ cup flour

1 teaspoon cinnamon
⅛ teaspoon nutmeg
2 tablespoons butter
Milk
Sugar and cinnamon

Prepare pastry for two-crust pie, using your favorite recipe. Line a 9–inch pie plate with bottom pastry crust; roll out top crust. In a large bowl, combine apple slices, sugar, flour, cinnamon, and nutmeg. Mix well. Spoon into lined pie plate, and dot with butter. Adjust top crust over filling, trimming excess pastry. Make several slits in top crust so steam can escape; then brush lightly with milk and sprinkle with sugar and cinnamon. Bake at 400 degrees for 45 minutes or until pastry is golden brown. Serves 6 to 8.

FRESH PEACH COBBLER

3 cups sliced fresh peaches	Dash of salt
⅔ cup sugar	½ cup sugar
¾ cup flour	¾ cup milk
2 teaspoons baking powder	½ cup butter

In a bowl, mix fresh peaches with ⅔ cup sugar and set aside for 30 minutes to 1 hour. In a separate bowl combine flour, baking powder, salt, and ½ cup sugar. Stir in milk. Melt butter in a 9 x 11–inch baking dish. Pour batter over melted butter; do not stir. Arrange peaches on top of batter. Bake at 350 degrees for 1 hour. Makes 6 to 8 servings.

PEEK-A-BERRY-BOO COOKIES

½ cup butter or margarine	2½ cups flour
½ cup shortening	1 teaspoon baking soda
1 cup brown sugar	1 teaspoon salt
¾ cup granulated sugar	½ teaspoon cinnamon
2 eggs	2 cups rolled oats
½ cup water	1 cup strawberry or blackberry jam
1 tablespoon vanilla	

Cream butter, shortening, sugars, and eggs. Stir in water and vanilla. Stir or sift together flour, baking soda, salt, and cinnamon. Add to creamed mixture, stirring until combined. Add rolled oats and mix well. Drop by teaspoonfuls on ungreased cookie sheet. Make a slight indentation in center of each cookie, and fill with 1 teaspoon jam. Top with ½ teaspoon of dough. Bake at 400 degrees for 10 minutes. Makes 4 dozen cookies.

APPLESAUCE COOKIES

1 cup sugar
½ cup butter
1 egg
1 cup thick applesauce
2 cups flour
1 teaspoon baking powder

1 teaspoon baking soda
1 teaspoon salt
1 teaspoon cinnamon
½ teaspoon cloves
1 cup raisins
1 cup chopped nuts

In a mixing bowl cream together sugar and butter. Add egg and applesauce. Sift together flour, baking powder, baking soda, salt, cinnamon, and cloves. Add to creamed mixture, mixing well. Stir in raisins and nuts. Drop by teaspoonfuls onto a greased cookie sheet. Bake at 350 degrees for 10 minutes. Makes 2 dozen cookies.

ENGLISH TOFFEE

2½ cups sugar
2 cups butter
½ cup water
3 tablespoons light corn syrup

1 cup slivered almonds
2 teaspoons vanilla
⅔ cup semisweet chocolate chips
½ cup ground almonds

In a heavy saucepan, combine sugar, butter, water, and corn syrup. Cover and bring to a boil. Remove cover and cook over medium heat until mixture turns golden, stirring frequently. Add slivered almonds, and continue cooking, stirring frequently, to about 300 degrees on a candy thermometer, or until a little of the candy, dropped into cold water, becomes hard and brittle. Remove from heat and add vanilla. Pour into an ungreased 13 x 9–inch pan. Sprinkle chocolate over hot candy, and cover with a sheet of aluminum foil to melt. Sprinkle with ground almonds. Makes approximately 2 pounds candy.

3 · CASTLE COUNTRY

Castle Country is home to a one-of-a-kind geologic formation: the San Rafael Swell. This unique red-rock oval-shaped uplift encompasses and borders scenic wonders such as Goblin Valley, Desolation Canyon, Labyrinth Canyon, and Windowblind Peak. In this enchanted arena, evidences of prehistoric life abound. More complete dinosaur skeletons have been excavated here than anywhere else in the United States. Designated a National Natural Landmark in 1966, the Cleveland Lloyd Dinosaur Quarry near Price is unique in the great numbers of bones that have been excavated (over twelve thousand bones from at least seventy different animals).

Human occupation of the San Rafael region dates back to the Archaic period, pre-dating even the Fremont culture that inhabited the area from A.D. 500 to 1300. The ancient people left some of the finest preserved petroglyphs and pictographs ever discovered. In addition, figurines and rock art panels, such as the well-known "Head Hunter," have been found.

The Ute Indians were the next peoples to make their home in Castle Country. Like many other tribes, they were dispersed as pioneer settlements were established. The first Europeans to enter the area were those who traveled along the Old Spanish Trail; however, it was not until the late 1870s that groups of Mormon pioneers established homesteads along the Price River and in Castle Valley. This rather desolate area also attracted those with lesser reputations: several infamous outlaws spent time hiding out in the deserts of Castle Country. In 1898, a shootout took place near Price, where a posse killed two outlaws, one said to be Butch Cassidy. At the viewing of the bodies, one lone man stood in the rear and snickered. As it turned out, the chuckling cowboy was none other than Cassidy himself, who must have enjoyed his "funeral" tremendously. The two outlaws are still buried in the Price Cemetery, with this story inscribed on their tombstone.

In the 1880s vast coal deposits were discovered and coal mining became a major industry in the region. Many immigrant workers were imported by the coal companies, giving the area a remarkable ethnic diversity. Helper became known as the town of "57 Varieties," and the Greek Orthodox Church is a major landmark in Price, the region's largest town. Coal mining brought not only wealth and diversity but also tragedy. In the early 1900s nearly five hundred miners were killed in two deadly explosions, and major strikes in 1903–4, 1922, and 1933 brought violence and eventual unionization to the mines. Today a major electricity-generation plant near Castle Dale provides close to 200 megawatts of electricity per year. With 98 percent of the power derived from coal, this industry remains very much alive.

Natural beauty and recreational attractions draw tens of thousands of visitors to Castle Country each year. The Green River, on the region's eastern border, is one of Utah's premier river-running areas. Mountain biking has also become a favorite sport: the San Rafael Swell is said to be the "ultimate fat-tire adventure" for cyclists.

In addition to the many outdoor activities, there is also intellectual and cultural stimulation. Price is home to the College of Eastern Utah, whose Prehistoric Museum houses an outstanding collection of dinosaur tracks (found in the local coal mines), a rare dinosaur egg, dinosaur skeletons, and a prehistoric Indian exhibit. A recent addition to the collection is a 10,000–year-old Columbian Mammoth, discovered nearby in 1988.

The ethnic diversity of Castle Country has given it a particularly interesting cuisine. A substantial Greek community has taken advantage of the area's large sheep herds for traditional lamb dishes and introduced such Greek specialties as dolmades, ratatouille, and baklava. Traditional cowboy fare, such as steak, home fries, and sourdough bread, is also popular in this area of many ranches. And Green River's annual Melon Days festival spotlights the queen of the local crop, represented in this book by melon chutney, cantaloupe and peach jam, and lemonade-watermelon punch.

DUTCH-OVEN LAMB FRY

5 pounds lamb chops or 3 pounds boneless loin of lamb	Lemon pepper
Vegetable oil for frying	Salt and pepper to taste

Cut lamb into 1½–inch cubes. Heat oil to boiling point in a Dutch oven or cast-iron skillet. Add lamb meat and fry, turning each piece over when it is brown, until meat is tender. Season while hot with lemon pepper, salt, and pepper. For extra tenderness, put browned meat in a large pan with a small amount of water, cover with lid, and steam to sweat the fat out.

Contributor's comments: "In June 1963 ground was broken for Joe's Valley Reservoir. To mark the occasion, refreshments were served to guests. Mark Humphrey, secretary-treasurer of the newly formed Emery Water Conservancy District, asked his wife, Merene, to prepare lamb (the Humphreys have a large herd of sheep) and scones. Guests consumed the food with gusto, and since then, lamb and scones have been served at Orangeville's annual July 24 Pioneer Day celebration. Members of the Humphrey family usually prepare the lamb. Others in the community, using the sourdough scone recipe developed by Merene, fry up large batches of scones, which are eaten with butter and honey or dipped in cinnamon and sugar. People come from miles around to enjoy the delicious meal."

MERENE'S SOURDOUGH SCONES

2 cups milk	2 teaspoons salt
6 tablespoons shortening	1½ cups Castle County Sourdough Starter (recipe follows)
½ package active dry yeast	6 cups flour (approximately)
3 tablespoons warm water	¾ teaspoon baking soda
1 tablespoon sugar	

In a large saucepan, scald the milk over medium heat. Remove pan from heat, and add shortening. Set aside to cool. In a small bowl, dissolve yeast in the warm water. To the cooled milk, add sugar, salt, and dissolved yeast. Stir in sourdough starter, 2 cups of the flour, and baking soda. Beat with mixer. Add remaining flour, a little at a time, mixing and kneading with hands until consistency of bread dough. Let rest for 10 minutes. Knead for about 10 minutes more. Place in a greased container, turning once to grease top of dough; cover and let rise until double in bulk. Roll dough to ½–inch thickness. Cut into rectangles approximately 2 x 3 inches, and place on oiled cookie sheet. Let rise until light. Deep fry in hot fat, turning once, until golden brown on both sides. Drain on paper towels. Serve with butter and honey or roll in mixture of granulated sugar and cinnamon. Makes 90 to 100 scones.

CASTLE COUNTRY SOURDOUGH STARTER

1 cup buttermilk   1 cup flour

Mix buttermilk and flour well and place in a glass or pottery container. Cover and let stand at room temperature for at least 48 hours, or until it starts to ferment and has a slightly sour odor. Store, tightly covered, in refrigerator. (Do not be concerned if the liquid starts to separate from the batter after it stands several days; stir only when removing starter or adding ingredients to replenish it.)

Each time you remove starter to add to a recipe, replenish it by adding equal parts of flour and evaporated milk (1 cup flour and 1 cup evaporated milk). Let stand in a warm place for at least 12 hours or until bubbly. Then cover tightly and return to refrigerator or freezer.

SOURDOUGH WAFFLES

½ cup Castle Country Sourdough
    Starter (recipe on page 53)
1 cup milk
1 cup warm water
1¾ cups flour

2 eggs
2 tablespoons sugar
½ teaspoon salt
1 teaspoon baking soda
¼ cup oil or melted shortening

In a large bowl, combine starter, milk, warm water, and flour; mix to blend. Cover bowl loosely and leave at room temperature overnight. The next day, add eggs, sugar, salt, baking soda, and oil or melted shortening; mix well. Bake in a hot waffle iron until golden brown. Makes 6 to 8 waffles.

SPRING LEG OF LAMB

1 leg of lamb, 3 to 5 pounds
Salt
1 large clove garlic, sliced
1 lemon, sliced

2 cups hot water
1 tablespoon Worcestershire sauce
2 tablespoons butter, melted
1 teaspoon oregano, crushed

Remove skin and fat from lamb; sprinkle with salt. Make slits in lamb and insert garlic slices. Preheat roasting pan in 400–degree oven. Place lamb in pan, return pan to oven, and sear lamb on all sides. Remove from oven and cover top of meat with lemon slices, fastened in place with toothpicks. Reduce oven temperature to 300 degrees. Combine water, Worcestershire sauce, melted butter, and oregano. Baste roast with sauce. Cover with lid, and return to oven. Baste several times as meat roasts, which will take about 2½ to 3 hours. To determine doneness, insert a meat thermometer into thickest part of leg; remove from oven when it registers 175 degrees for medium or 180 degrees for well done.

LAMB AND EGGPLANT CASSEROLE

1 pound lamb stew meat, cut in
    ½–inch cubes
2 small onions, sliced
¼ cup oil
1 small eggplant, pared and sliced
Salt and pepper to taste
1 can (14 ounces) green beans,
    drained
2 medium carrots, sliced

1 green pepper, cut in rings
4 medium tomatoes, peeled and
    sliced
Salt and pepper to taste
2 cups cooked rice
1 cup shredded cheddar cheese
Paprika
Snipped fresh parsley

In a large skillet, brown lamb and onions in oil until tender. Drain. Arrange eggplant in a greased 13 x 9-inch baking dish. Top with lamb and onions. Layer beans, carrots, green pepper, and tomato slices on lamb; sprinkle with salt and pepper. Cover and bake at 350 degrees for 1 hour. Remove from oven and arrange rice in 4 diagonal strips (using half a cupful for each strip) on top of casserole. Sprinkle with cheese and paprika. Bake, uncovered, until cheese is melted, about 15 minutes. Sprinkle with parsley. Makes 10 to 12 servings.

SAVORY MARINATED STEAK

⅓ cup vegetable oil
⅓ cup lemon juice
1 teaspoon grated lemon rind
3 tablespoons Worcestershire sauce
1 clove garlic, minced

1 teaspoon salt
1 teaspoon rosemary, crumbled
¼ teaspoon freshly ground pepper
6 to 8 beef steaks

Combine oil, lemon juice and grated rind, Worcestershire sauce, garlic, salt, rosemary, and pepper in a covered jar and shake to blend well. Chill 1 hour or more to blend flavors. Half an hour before grilling meat, baste meat with marinade. Baste two or three times while grilling. Makes 6 to 8 servings.

CHICKEN RISOTTO

1 broiler-fryer chicken (3 to 4
    pounds), cut up
¼ cup olive oil
1 medium onion, chopped
1 medium green pepper, chopped

1½ cups uncooked rice
2 cloves garlic, minced
Salt and pepper to taste
1 can (16 ounces) tomatoes, diced
3 cups water or chicken broth

In an oven roaster pan, brown chicken pieces in olive oil. Add onion and green pepper, and sauté until vegetables are tender. Stir in rice, garlic, salt, and pepper. Pour tomatoes and broth over chicken and rice mixture. Stir well. Cover and bake at 350 degrees for 1 hour or until rice is tender and moisture is absorbed. Add water if needed. Makes 6 to 8 servings.

PAGEANT POTATOES AU GRATIN

8 to 10 medium potatoes
1 cup butter or margarine
1 cup milk
2 cups shredded cheddar cheese

1 teaspoon celery salt
Salt and pepper to taste
Snipped fresh parsley

In a large pot, boil potatoes with skins on until tender. Remove from heat, drain, and cool. Peel and slice potatoes and place them in a greased 3–quart casserole dish. Set aside. In a heavy saucepan, melt butter. Add milk and cheese, and stir over medium heat until smooth. Add celery salt, salt, and pepper. Pour sauce over sliced potatoes. Bake, uncovered, at 350 degrees for 40 minutes. Sprinkle with parsley and serve. Makes 8 to 10 servings.

POLENTA WITH SAUSAGE SAUCE

1 to 2 pounds Italian sausage
2 tablespoons olive oil
1 medium onion, chopped
1 clove garlic, chopped
1 can (6 ounces) tomato paste
1½ cups water
2 cans (8 ounces each) tomato sauce

½ teaspoon black pepper
¼ teaspoon red hot pepper
6 cups water
1 teaspoon salt
2 cups cornmeal
Parmesan cheese

Prepare sauce: Cut sausage into small pieces, and fry in hot olive oil until brown. Remove grease, then sauté onion and garlic. Combine tomato paste and 1½ cups water. Stir diluted tomato paste, tomato sauce, black pepper, and red pepper into sausage mixture. Cover and simmer for 1 hour; check occasionally, adding water if needed so sauce remains moist.

Prepare polenta: In a large, heavy saucepan, bring 5 cups water to a boil. Add salt and remaining 1 cup cold water. Stir in cornmeal slowly with a wire whisk, and stir continually over medium heat until smooth and thick, about 2 minutes. Remove from heat and prepare casserole immediately (polenta will too become thick if it is allowed to cool).

Prepare casserole: In a 4-quart greased baking dish, layer polenta with sauce, ending with sauce on top. Sprinkle with Parmesan cheese. Cover and bake at 350 degrees for 30 minutes. Makes 8 to 10 servings.

DOLMADES (STUFFED GRAPEVINE LEAVES)

1 jar (16 ounces) grapevine leaves
1 pound ground beef or lamb
1 medium onion, chopped
2 tablespoons chopped parsley
1 teaspoon Greek seasoning

1 teaspoon salt
Pepper to taste
⅓ cup long-grain rice, uncooked
2 cans (14½ ounces each) chicken
   broth

Rinse grapevine leaves. Cover with water in a saucepan and bring to a boil. Drain and rinse again. Set aside. In a medium skillet, brown ground beef. Add chopped onion and parsley and cook until onions are tender. Stir in Greek seasoning, salt, pepper, rice, and ⅓ cup chicken broth (set remaining chicken broth aside). Cook for 5 minutes. Place a heaping teaspoon of meat mixture at stem end of each grapevine leaf, vein side up. Fold sides of leaf in and roll tightly toward point into oblong shape. In a saucepan, arrange stuffed leaves, seam side down, close together in layers. Cover with remaining chicken broth. Place an oven-proof plate over dolmades to prevent leaves from opening. Cover saucepan, and cook over medium-low heat for 1 hour, until leaves are tender. Drain broth before removing plate. Makes approximately 20 dolmades.

GREEN RIVER MELON CHUTNEY

1½ cups cubed cantaloupe
1½ cups cubed honeydew melon
2 cups sugar
⅔ cup white vinegar
¼ cup currants

½ cup finely chopped onion
½ cup finely chopped red bell pepper
1 teaspoon cinnamon
¼ teaspoon ground cloves

Combine all ingredients in a large saucepan. Bring to boil over medium heat. Reduce heat and simmer, uncovered, about 30 minutes or till slightly thickened. Pour into sterilized hot jars and seal, or allow to cool and serve. Makes 2 pints.

GNOCCHI (POTATO DUMPLINGS) WITH CHEESE

2 pounds baking potatoes, peeled
    and cubed
1 tablespoon olive oil
½ teaspoon salt
1 egg

2 cups flour
½ cup butter or olive oil
¼ cup grated Parmesan or Romano
    cheese

Boil potato cubes 10 to 15 minutes or until tender. Drain. Add olive oil and salt, and mash. Cool. Stir in egg. Add flour and mix into a soft dough. Divide dough into 4 portions. On a floured board, form each piece of dough into a rope about ¾ inch in diameter. Cut into 1–inch pieces, and roll each piece on the rough side of a vegetable grater or back of a fork to give it design and texture. Dust with flour and set on tray to dry. When ready to serve, bring 8 quarts water to a boil. Add one-third of the dough pieces, or gnocchi, to water; boil until gnocchi float to the top. Continue boiling for 1 minute. Remove with a strainer. Repeat with remaining gnocchi. Toss with butter or olive oil and cheese. Makes 6 to 8 servings.

WATERMELON RIND RELISH

4 quarts watermelon rind, peeled
    and grated
2 cups diced red bell peppers
1 cup diced onion
2¼ cups (1 pound) light brown
    sugar
1 cup cider vinegar

1 teaspoon salt
1 teaspoon fennel seeds
1 teaspoon mustard seeds
¼ teaspoon red pepper flakes
10 whole cloves
1 3–inch cinnamon stick

In a 6–quart enamel or stainless steel pot, combine all ingredients; mix well. Bring to a boil, then reduce heat and simmer until thick, stirring occasionally. Pour into sterilized jars and seal, or chill and serve. Makes 10 pints.

RATATOUILLE

2 tablespoons olive oil
3 large onions, chopped
4 green peppers, cut in bite-size
    chunks
1 small eggplant, peeled* and cubed
3 garlic cloves, chopped

4 small zucchini, peeled* and cubed
5 medium tomatoes, quartered, or 1
    can (14½ ounces) tomatoes,
    drained
Salt and pepper to taste
Parmesan cheese

Heat skillet, then add oil. Sauté onion, green pepper, and eggplant. Stir in garlic, zucchini, tomatoes, and salt and pepper to taste. Cover pan and cook over low heat until vegetables are tender, about 10 minutes. (If vegetables give off too much liquid, cook last few minutes uncovered.) Just before serving, sprinkle with Parmesan cheese. Makes 6 to 8 servings.

*Note: If eggplant and zucchini are young and have tender skins, do not peel.

TORTELLINI SALAD

1 cup chopped fresh broccoli
1 package (12 ounces) cheese-filled
    tortellini
1 package (10 ounces) frozen peas
¼ teaspoon salt
⅛ teaspoon pepper
1 small red onion, chopped

1 can (8 ounces) water chestnuts,
    chopped
½ cup pine nuts or slivered almonds
1 cup olive oil
½ cup red wine vinegar
1 garlic clove, crushed

In a small saucepan, steam broccoli until tender; drain well and set aside until cool. In a 4–quart pot, bring 2 quarts water to boil. Stir in tortellini, peas, salt, and pepper; boil, uncovered, until tortellini is cooked, about 15 to 20 minutes. Remove from heat and drain well. Place in a large serving bowl and set aside until cool. Combine tortellini with broccoli, red onion, water chestnuts, and nuts. Place olive oil, vinegar, and garlic in a jar or other covered container. Shake well. Pour desired amount of dressing over tortellini; refrigerate for 2 hours before serving. Makes 6 to 8 servings.

Lemonade and Watermelon Punch (p. 69); Fresh Corn Salad (p. 190); Aunt Iris's Rolls (p. 123); Grandmother Stoker's Baked Beans (p. 119); Moroni's Famous Barbecued Turkey (p. 184).

Clockwise from top left: Scandinavian Wheat Bread (p. 193); Manti Whole Wheat Bread (p. 193); Alice's Navajo Fry Bread (p. 37); Mormon Muffins (p. 124); Sourdough Biscuits (p. 104); State Fair Muffins (p. 103); Easter Bread (p. 63); Raspberry Jelly (p. 23).

EASTER BREAD

4 to 5 cups flour
½ cup sugar
1 teaspoon salt
1 package (1 tablespoon) active dry
    yeast
½ cup warm water
¼ cup milk
½ cup butter or margarine

3 eggs at room temperature
1 tablespoon anise extract
¼ teaspoon nutmeg
5 eggs
Confectioners'-sugar frosting
1 tablespoon grated lemon or orange
    peel

In a large bowl, mix 1 cup flour, sugar, salt, and yeast. In a saucepan, combine water, milk, and butter or margarine; heat until warm, about 125 degrees. Pour over dry ingredients and beat until smooth. Add 3 eggs, one at a time, anise extract, and nutmeg. Beat well. Gradually add enough remaining flour to make a soft dough. Turn out on a floured board and knead lightly or until dough is smooth and elastic. Place in a greased bowl. Cover and let rise until doubled in bulk, about 1 hour.

While dough is rising, dye 5 uncooked eggs with Easter egg dyes, following package directions, or food coloring stirred into very hot water. Set aside.

Punch down risen dough and divide into 3 equal pieces. On a floured board, form each piece into a rope about 18 inches long and 2 inches in diameter. Place ropes side by side on greased cookie sheet and braid them loosely together. Put one of the colored eggs in each twist. Let rise in a warm place for 1 hour. Bake at 350 degrees for 30 to 35 minutes or until golden brown. If desired, frost with confectioners'-sugar frosting and garnish with lemon or orange peel.

Note: This is a favorite bread in both Italian and Greek cultures.

FEATHER ROLLS

2 packages (2 tablespoons) active
    dry yeast
½ cup warm water
1 tablespoon sugar
1 cup milk

⅓ cup butter or margarine, melted
⅓ cup sugar
2 teaspoons salt
2 eggs, beaten
4 to 5 cups flour

Dissolve yeast in warm water with 1 tablespoon sugar. Scald milk over medium heat; add melted butter or margarine, ⅓ cup sugar, salt, eggs, and yeast mixture. Stir in flour and mix well (dough will be sticky). Refrigerate overnight. (If you prefer to bake rolls same day you mix them, add a little more flour and knead well. Then proceed with remaining steps.) When ready to use, pull off pieces of dough and shape into rolls; place on a greased cookie sheet. Cover lightly with a clean dishtowel and allow to rise at least 2 hours. Bake at 425 degrees for 10 minutes. Makes 20 to 24 rolls.

Contributor's comments: "I like to pull off roll-size pieces of dough and roll them on a floured board rope-like, then tie them into knots. Let knot-shaped rolls rise as directed, then bake."

GREEK FESTIVAL LOUKOMADES

2 cups milk
¼ cup butter or margarine
1 teaspoon salt
3 tablespoons sugar
2 eggs
1 package (1 tablespoon) yeast

1 cup warm water
5 cups flour
Oil for deep-frying
1 cup honey
½ cup sugar
1 teaspoon cinnamon

In a heavy saucepan over medium heat, scald milk with butter. Cool. Add salt, 3 tablespoons sugar, and eggs. In a small bowl, dissolve yeast in water, then add to milk mixture. Add flour to liquid mixture 1 cup at a time, mixing well after each addition. Cover dough and let rise until double in bulk. Drop dough by teaspoonfuls into hot oil. Deep-fry, turning once, until golden on each side. Drizzle with honey, and sprinkle with combined sugar and cinnamon. Makes 4 dozen.

BAKLAVA

1 pound phyllo (available in frozen-
    food section of grocery store)
2 pounds walnuts, chopped
¼ cup sugar
½ teaspoon cinnamon
2 cups butter, melted

2 cups sugar
1 cup water
7 tablespoons honey
½ lemon
Whole cloves

Mix chopped nuts, ¼ cup sugar, and cinnamon. Melt butter in a saucepan. Butter an 11½ x 13–inch baking pan. Layer 4 or 5 sheets of phyllo on pan, buttering each sheet as it is added. Spread with thin layer of walnut mixture. Add another buttered sheet of phyllo and another layer of walnut mixture; continue layering in this manner until walnut mixture is used up. Then cover with 5 to 7 sheets of phyllo, buttering each one as it is added. Cut into 2–inch diamond shapes. Firmly place 1 clove into center of each diamond, to hold phyllo sheets in place. Bake at 425 degrees for 2 to 5 minutes. Reduce oven temperature to 350 degrees, and bake 1 hour or until golden brown.

As soon as baklava is in oven, prepare syrup: Squeeze juice from lemon and remove seeds. In a large saucepan, combine 2 cups sugar, 1 cup water, honey, and lemon juice. Add remaining pulp and rind of lemon. Boil for approximately 12 minutes (start timing after mixture comes to a boil), stirring constantly, or until a fine string forms when spoon is removed from syrup (softball stage, or about 240 degrees on a candy thermometer). Remove from heat and discard lemon rind. Set syrup aside to cool.

Remove baklava from oven and spoon on syrup while still hot. Cool, then serve. Makes 24 pieces.

ITALIAN SCALLIES (COOKIES)

12 eggs
1 cup sugar
¼ teaspoon salt
1 cup vegetable oil
1 teaspoon vanilla
1 teaspoon anise extract
6 cups flour

2 cups honey
3 tablespoons orange juice
    concentrate, thawed
½ teaspoon anise extract
Oil for deep-frying
Sugar

In a large bowl, beat eggs. Add sugar, salt, and oil; blend. Add vanilla, 1 teaspoon anise extract, and flour and stir to a moderately stiff dough, resembling pastry. Roll dough rope-like on a floured board, and cut in 6–inch lengths. Twist each piece of dough into a circle, like a doughnut, or tie in a knot. Deep-fry in hot oil, turning once, until golden on each side. Cool.

In a saucepan, combine honey, orange juice concentrate, and ½ teaspoon anise extract; bring to a boil. Dip cooled cookies into honey mixture until covered. Place on wire rack to drain. Sprinkle with granulated sugar. Makes 4 dozen.

BISCOTTI (ITALIAN COOKIES)

6 eggs
1 cup sugar
½ teaspoon salt
5 tablespoons butter, melted

2 teaspoons anise extract
3¾ cups flour
2½ tablespoons baking powder
1 cup toasted whole almonds

In a large mixing bowl, beat eggs. Add sugar, salt, melted butter, and anise extract. Stir in flour, baking powder, and toasted almonds. Mix together to form a soft dough. On a floured board, shape dough into a loaf 12 inches long and 3 to 4 inches wide; place loaf on a greased cookie sheet. Bake at 350 degrees for 20 minutes. Remove from oven. Cut into 1–inch slices and return to cookie sheet. Bake for an additional 20 minutes, until slices are toasted. Makes 2 dozen cookies.

CASTLE VALLEY JELLY ROLL

4 eggs, separated	1½ teaspoons baking powder
3 tablespoons water	2 tablespoons cornstarch
1 cup sugar	Confectioners' sugar
1 cup plus 1 tablespoon flour	Jelly

Grease and line with wax paper a 10½ x 15½ x 1–inch jelly-roll pan. Set aside. In a mixing bowl, beat egg yolks and water until thick. Add sugar and mix well. Sift flour, baking powder, and cornstarch together; fold into yolk mixture. Set aside. In a separate bowl, beat egg whites until they form a stiff peak. Gently fold into yolk mixture. Pour batter into prepared jelly-roll pan. Bake at 325 degrees for about 13 minutes, until light brown.

Lightly dust a clean dish towel with confectioners' sugar. Remove cake from oven, loosen edges, and invert onto dish towel. Carefully peel off paper. With sharp knife, cut crisp edges from cake. Roll up cake gently from narrow end, rolling towel in it to prevent cake's sticking. Cool about 10 minutes.

Unroll cake (leaving it on towel) and spread with jelly to within ½ inch of edges. Start rolling up cake from narrow end; continue rolling, lifting towel higher and higher with one hand as you guide the roll with the other. Finish with open end of cake on underside. Wrap tightly in wax paper and place on wire rack until completely cool. To serve, cut into 1–inch slices. Makes 8 to 10 servings.

FIESTA CAKE

7 to 8 egg whites (1 cup)
1 teaspoon cream of tartar
1 teaspoon salt
¾ cup sugar
1¼ cups flour

¾ cup sugar
¼ cup cold water
1 tablespoon lemon juice
1 teaspoon vanilla
8 to 9 egg yolks (½ cup)

In a large mixing bowl, beat egg whites and cream of tartar until foamy; then gradually add salt and ¾ cup sugar, beating continually until mixture stands in stiff peaks. In a separate mixing bowl, combine flour and ¾ cup sugar. Make a well in center of flour mixture and add remaining ingredients. Beat until thick and light in color.

Carefully fold egg-yolk mixture into beaten egg whites. Pour into ungreased angel food cake pan. Carefully run a knife through batter to remove air bubbles. Bake at 350 degrees for 50 to 55 minutes. Remove from oven and immediately turn upside down. Cool completely. Loosen edges of cake with knife, and remove from pan. Frost with a glaze, or serve with fruit and sweetened whipped cream or other whipped topping.

AMERICAN ICE CREAM

1½ cups milk
1 cup sugar
1 tablespoon cornstarch
¼ teaspoon salt

2 eggs, beaten
½ cup milk
3 cups heavy cream
2 teaspoons vanilla

In a heavy saucepan, combine 1½ cups milk, sugar, cornstarch, and salt; stir over medium heat for 15 minutes. Mix eggs with ½ cup milk and add to hot mixture. Continue stirring constantly over medium heat until mixture coats the back of a metal spoon, about 3 minutes. Remove from heat and cool. Add cream and vanilla. Pour into a 4–quart ice-cream freezer. Freeze and pack according to manufacturer's instructions. Makes 10 to 12 servings.

LEMONADE AND WATERMELON PUNCH

1 large watermelon (about 25
   pounds)
1 can (12 ounces) frozen lemonade
   concentrate, thawed
2 cups water

¼ cup grenadine syrup
1 to 2 bottles (32 ounces each)
   lemon-lime carbonated soda,
   chilled

Select a watermelon about 20 inches long with a flat base. The day before serving, cut an 8–inch oval section out of the top of the melon, making a sawtooth edge,. Remove cut portion and reserve. Using a long-handled spoon, scoop out all the melon pulp; remove seeds. Place about ¼ of the pulp in a blender container or food processor; cover and blend till pureed. Repeat with remaining pulp. Place melon shell on tray. Return puree to melon shell, and stir in lemonade concentrate, water, and grenadine. Replace cut portion of melon; refrigerate overnight. Just before serving, remove cut portion of melon. Stir in lemon-lime soda until shell is ¾ full. Makes about 20 servings.

MARK'S FAMOUS HONEY TAFFY

2 cups sugar
¼ cup butter
½ cup honey

½ cup water
Pinch of salt

In a heavy saucepan, combine all ingredients. Cook, stirring constantly, until sugar is dissolved. Then cook over medium-high heat, stirring as little as possible, to 260 degrees on candy thermometer, or until a little mixture, dropped into cold water, forms a hard ball. Remove from heat and pour onto buttered shallow pan or platter to cool. When cool enough to handle, pull with buttered fingers until taffy is satin smooth and ropy. Cut into bite-size pieces with buttered scissors, and wrap in wax paper, if desired. Makes 1½ pounds candy.

CANTALOUPE AND PEACH JAM

3½ cups pureed cantaloupe
½ cup chopped or mashed peaches
1 package (1.75 ounces) powdered
    pectin

¼ cup fresh lemon juice
6 cups sugar
¼ teaspoon margarine

In a heavy saucepan, combine cantaloupe, peaches, pectin, and lemon juice; bring to a rolling boil. Stir in sugar, and bring to a rolling boil again. Add margarine, and return to a rolling boil. Continue to boil for 4 minutes. Pour into sterilized jars and seal. Makes 6 to 7½ pints.

Variations: Instead of peaches, use ½ cup of one of the following: blueberries, strawberries, raspberries, blackberries, or crushed pineapple.

Contributor's comments: "The Green River area is well-known for its delicious melons. In my grandfather's day, the farmers would often store the melons in their haystacks to protect them from freezing, giving them delicious melons to eat in the late fall and early winter. My grandfather, Joseph Laramie Allen, was one of many farmers whose melons were shipped by train across the country."

4 · COLOR COUNTRY

Color Country, in the southwestern part of Utah, boasts one of the greatest concentrations of national parks and forests in the United States. Within this area are three national parks—Zion, Bryce Canyon, and Capitol Reef—and a small portion of a fourth, Canyonlands; Cedar Breaks National Monument; the two-million-acre Dixie National Forest; part of Fish Lake National Forest; and an additional six million acres of nationally protected land. State parks also abound, including Coral Pink Sand Dunes, Gunlock, Snow Canyon, Anasazi Indian Village, Escalante, Kodachrome Basin, Iron Mission, Minersville, and Quail Creek.

Native Americans roamed Color Country more than ten thousand years ago. Two Indian cultures, the Anasazi and the Fremont, constructed granaries and pit houses in the area as early as A.D. 1250. Remnants of these cultures can be seen today in preserved ruin sites and petroglyphs throughout the region and in the artifacts collection at the Anasazi Indian Village State Park near Boulder. More recently, the Southern Paiutes and the Ute Indians resided in the area. Though most of the Indian culture is now history, their traditions live on through the tribal headquarters of today's Southern Paiute Indian Reservation in Cedar City.

The earliest documented evidence of early Spanish exploration in southern Utah dates to 1776, the year the American colonies declared independence from England. That year an expedition led by two Franciscan missionaries, Francisco Atanasio Dominguez and Silvestre Velez de Escalante, entered what is now Utah while searching for an overland route from New Mexico to California. They entered southeastern Utah, traveled as far north as the Great Salt Lake, then headed southwest in late September. Because of early snowstorms, they decided not to go on to California, but started heading back to Santa Fe after reaching the Grand Canyon. Their detailed diary provided the first description of southwestern Utah.

Anglo-Americans first visited the area in 1826, when an expedition led by Jedediah S. Smith passed through southwestern Utah while en route to southern California. Within three years of the 1847 arrival of Brigham Young and the early Mormon pioneers in the Salt Lake Valley, families were sent to southern Utah to test the area's agricultural potential. By the 1860s, hundreds of families were raising cotton, figs, grapes, olives, sugar, and almonds in permanent settlements.

In the 1870s silver mining became a key industry for several locations in Color Country. Most mining booms survived less than a decade, but the mines were profitable while they lasted. Enormous coal reserves were also discovered, and coal mining continues to be important to the region's economic growth.

The twentieth century has brought far-reaching changes to Color Country. Zion National Park and Bryce Canyon National Park were established, bringing tourism to the region. During the Great Depression in the 1930s, Civilian Conservation Corps workers constructed roads, reseeded forests, installed telephone lines, and built ranger stations and hiking trails. The twenties and thirties also gave rise to what became known as "Little Hollywood," as Western filmmakers discovered the rugged scenery following the success of 1922's *Deadwood Coach,* starring Tom Mix.

Today Color Country's economy depends on a wide variety of industries. There is still lots of ranching, mining, lumbering, agriculture, and movie making, but new industries are also moving into the region. Millions of tourists are still drawn each year to the national and state parks and forests, but they also come to attend performances at the Utah Shakespearean Festival at Southern Utah State University in Cedar City and at Tuacahn, a spectacular arts complex near St. George; to ski at Brian Head resort; to fish in mountain lakes, rivers, and streams; to hunt game animals, such as elk and deer; and to observe unusual wildlife, such as the buffalo of the nation's only free-roaming herd, found in the Henry Mountains south of Hanksville.

The region's climate—ranging from mild to hot summers in the southwestern corner, Utah's Dixie, to mild but short summers and below-zero winter temperatures in the high mountains—lends itself well to some unusual foods. Two desert plants, the pomegranate and the prickly pear cactus, have provided moisture to save the lives of persons stranded in the hot deserts of Washington County. The colorful seeds of the pomegranate add interest to fruit cups, salads, and desserts, while pomegranate juice, used to flavor grenadine, is the basis for jellies, syrups, and beverages. Prickly pears, or cactus apples, make delicious jelly. Rhubarb is another indigenous plant, a vegetable that is usually used more as a fruit in pies and jams. And bountiful harvests of pecans provide nutty additions to pies, cakes, cookies, and candies.

BUFFALO OR BEEF POT ROAST

4 pounds buffalo or beef chuck roast	8 small potatoes, pared and halved
¼ cup flour	8 medium carrots, halved crosswise
1 tablespoon salt	and lengthwise
1¼ teaspoons pepper	8 small onions
2 tablespoons shortening	½ teaspoon salt
1 jar (5 ounces) horseradish	Gravy (recipe below)

Sift together flour, 1 tablespoon salt, and pepper; rub mixture on meat thoroughly. Melt shortening in a large skillet or Dutch oven; brown meat over medium heat about 15 minutes. Reduce heat. Spread horseradish on both sides of meat, and add 1 cup water to pan. Cover tightly and simmer on top of range or in 275–degree oven for 4 to 5 hours, until meat is tender. About 1 hour before end of cooking time, add potatoes, carrots, and onions, and sprinkle with ½ teaspoon salt. When meat and vegetables are tender, place on platter and cover with heavy foil to keep warm while making gravy. Slice meat and serve with gravy and vegetables. Makes 6 to 8 servings.

GRAVY FOR POT ROAST

Pour drippings (fat and juices) from the pot roast into a bowl, leaving brown particles in pan. Let fat rise to top of drippings; skim off fat, reserving ¼ cup. Place reserved fat in pan. Blend in ¼ cup all-purpose flour. Cook over low heat, stirring until mixture is smooth and bubbly. Remove from heat. Measure meat juice; add water to measure 2 cups liquid, and stir into flour mixture. Heat to boiling, stirring constantly. Boil and stir 1 minute. Season to taste with salt and pepper.

CHICKEN STEW AND DUMPLINGS

1 broiler-fryer chicken (about 4 pounds)	Salt to taste
1 onion, chopped	4 cups water
1 cup sliced celery	¼ cup flour
2 cups sliced carrots	½ cup cold water
8 peppercorns	2 cups fresh or frozen green peas
	Dumplings (recipe below)

Wash and dry chicken. Put chicken, onion, celery, carrots, peppercorns, salt, and 4 cups water in large pot. Bring to boil and skim broth; then reduce heat to low and cook, covered, until chicken is tender. Remove chicken from stock; discard skin and bones. Cut meat into large pieces. Remove vegetables from broth. Cool broth and skim fat as it rises to the top. Return broth to boiling. Blend flour with ½ cup cold water; add to boiling broth. Boil, stirring constantly, until thick. Return cooked vegetables and peas to broth; simmer until peas are tender. Return chicken to stew. Prepare dumplings (recipe below), and proceed as directed.

DUMPLINGS

1½ cups flour	1 egg, slightly beaten
2 teaspoons baking powder	½ cup milk
½ teaspoon salt	2 tablespoons shortening, melted
1 teaspoon parsley flakes	

Sift together flour, baking powder, and salt. Add parsley flakes. Combine egg, milk, and melted shortening. Add to flour mixture and mix only until moist. Drop by spoonfuls on top of the boiling chicken stew. Cover and simmer for 12 to 15 minutes; do not remove lid during cooking time. Makes 6 to 8 servings.

PANGUITCH POTATO CASSEROLE

4 pounds potatoes	1 cup (8 ounces) sour cream
¾ pound cheddar cheese, grated	⅔ cup buttermilk
½ cup chopped onion	Salt and pepper to taste

Wash and peel potatoes; boil just until tender. Drain and let potatoes cool slightly. Grate potatoes and add cheese, onion, sour cream, buttermilk, salt, and pepper, mixing lightly until just blended. Pour into 2–quart buttered casserole dish. Bake at 300 degrees for 1 hour. Makes 6 to 8 servings.

Contributor's comment: "Panguitch has a homecoming celebration each year on Pioneer Day, July 24. A highlight of the day is a pit-barbecued beef dinner, which is served to several hundred people. A few years ago my husband was in charge of the dinner. I had made this potato casserole for our family the day before the planning meeting, so he suggested that we serve it at the celebration instead of the usual baked potatoes. This casserole has become as traditional for the dinner as the barbecued beef."

GRAM'S ZUCCHINI DELIGHT

2 large potatoes, peeled and sliced	2 large zucchini, sliced
1 medium onion, sliced	Salt and pepper
⅓ cup butter or margarine	

In a large skillet, fry potatoes and onions in butter or margarine over medium heat for 5 to 7 minutes. Add zucchini and cook, stirring constantly, until vegetables are tender. Add salt and pepper to taste. Makes 4 to 6 servings.

PANGUITCH SANDWICH

1 can (6 ounces) salmon or tuna
1 cup grated cheddar cheese
3 hard-cooked eggs, chopped
3 tablespoons grated green bell
  pepper
3 tablespoons chopped onion

3 tablespoons finely chopped sweet
  pickle
3 tablespoons chopped ripe olives
Mayonnaise or salad dressing
Bread, buns, or rolls

Combine salmon or tuna, cheese, eggs, green pepper, onions, pickle, and olives. Add enough mayonnaise or salad dressing to moisten. Spread on bread and heat under the broiler until slightly browned, or stuff into buns or rolls, wrap in foil, and heat in 350–degree oven for 15 minutes. Makes 4 to 6 servings.

Contributor's comment: "During the 1950s, school-lunch programs received surplus salmon. One of the school-lunch cooks in Panguitch developed this recipe, entered it in a national contest, and won a trip to South America. Each time I bake bread, I roll out some of the dough and make biscuits, cut into rounds with a tuna can, to use for sandwiches. This is one of our favorite fillings."

APPLESAUCE SPICE CAKE

½ cup butter or shortening
1 cup sugar
1 egg
1½ cups applesauce
4 tablespoons hot water
2½ cups flour

1 teaspoon baking soda
1 teaspoon cinnamon
1 teaspoon cloves
1 teaspoon salt
1 cup raisins
½ cup nuts, chopped

Cream together butter or shortening, sugar, and egg. Add applesauce and hot water. Stir or sift together flour, baking soda, cinnamon, cloves, and salt; add to creamed mixture. Add raisins and nuts. Mix well. Pour into a greased and floured 9 x 13–inch pan. Bake at 350 degrees for 45 minutes, or until cake tests done.

ANGEL FOOD CAKE

Whites of 1 dozen eggs

1½ teaspoons cream of tartar

1½ teaspoons vanilla

½ teaspoon almond extract

¼ teaspoon salt

1 cup granulated sugar

1 cup flour

1 cup confectioners' sugar

In a large bowl and using an electric mixer, beat egg whites, cream of tartar, vanilla, almond extract, and salt at high speed until well mixed. Continue beating at high speed while gradually adding granulated sugar. Beat until sugar is dissolved and whites stand in peaks. Do not scrape side of bowl while beating. Sift together flour and confectioners' sugar. Using rubber spatula, fold dry ingredients into egg-white mixture about one-fourth at a time, folding over several times until each addition is incorporated. After flour has all been folded in, give batter a few more strokes to be sure it is well mixed. Gently pour into an ungreased 10–inch tube pan. With metal knife or spatula, cut through batter once, without lifting spatula out of batter, to break large air bubbles. Bake at 350 degrees for 35 minutes or until cake springs back when lightly touched. Invert cake in pan to cool. Cool completely before removing from pan.

Contributor's comment: "Springtime, when the chickens are laying and there are plenty of eggs, is a good time to make this cake. I don't always wait for spring to make it, though, because my family enjoys it so much. We like it with sweetened berries and whipped cream or just plain."

BEST FRUITCAKE

2 cups flour
2 teaspoons baking powder
½ teaspoon salt
1 pound candied pineapple, coarsely
    cut
1 pound candied cherries

1 pound dates, halved
4 eggs
1 cup sugar
1 pound pecan halves
2 tablespoons light corn syrup

Stir or sift together flour, baking powder, and salt. Stir in pineapple, cherries, and dates. In a separate bowl, beat eggs. Add sugar and mix until smooth. Stir into fruit mixture. Add pecans, and mix lightly. Pour batter into 2 greased and floured 7 x 4 x 2–inch loaf pans. Bake at 275 degrees for 1 hour. While fruitcake is still warm, brush with corn syrup. Makes 2 loaves.

RHUBARB CUSTARD PIE

Pastry for two-crust pie
3 eggs
3 tablespoons milk
2 cups sugar

3 tablespoons uncooked tapioca
4 cups diced rhubarb
2 tablespoons butter

Prepare pastry using favorite recipe. Roll out half the dough and line pie tin; roll out remaining dough for top crust. Beat eggs slightly; add milk. Mix sugar and tapioca together, and stir into milk and egg mixture. Put rhubarb in pastry-lined pan. Pour egg mixture over the top, and dot with butter. Cover with top pastry; trim and seal edges. Make holes in top for steam to escape. Bake at 350 degrees for 45 to 50 minutes, until lightly browned. Makes 6 to 8 servings.

Contributor's comment: "In grandmother's day rhubarb was considered a 'spring tonic.' Although it is technically a vegetable, it is usually used as a fruit. To get it growing early in the spring, one of my friends covers it with a cardboard box. She always says that rhubarb is like love: the more you give away, the more you have. Rhubarb grows best when picked often."

DIXIE PECAN PIE

Pastry for one-crust pie
¼ cup butter
1 cup sugar
3 eggs, beaten slightly

¾ cup light or dark corn syrup
¼ teaspoon salt
1 teaspoon vanilla
1 to 1½ cups chopped pecans

Prepare pastry using favorite recipe and line a pie tin. Cream butter and sugar until light and fluffy. Add eggs, corn syrup, salt, vanilla, and pecans. Blend well. Pour mixture in unbaked pastry shell. Bake at 375 degrees for 40 to 45 minutes, or until knife inserted in center comes out clean. Cool, then serve plain or with sweetened whipped cream. Makes 6 to 8 servings.

SHAKESPEARE STORYBOOK TARTS

1½ cups flour
¼ teaspoon salt
½ cup shortening
¼ cup ice-cold water
1 cup sugar
2 tablespoons butter or margarine

2 eggs
¼ cup evaporated milk
2 tablespoons lemon juice
2 cups raisins
½ cup walnuts, chopped

Prepare tart shells: Combine flour and salt in a mixing bowl. Cut shortening into flour. Add ice-cold water, and mix well. Roll out pastry; cut into large rounds and line muffin tins.

In a mixing bowl, cream sugar and butter or margarine. Beat in eggs one at a time. Add evaporated milk, lemon juice, raisins, and nuts. Spoon into unbaked tart shells. Bake at 350 degrees for 40 minutes, or until knife inserted in center of filling comes out clean. Makes 12 tarts.

CHOCOLATE WAFFLE-IRON COOKIES

3 squares unsweetened chocolate
1 cup butter or margarine
4 eggs
1½ cups sugar
2 cups flour

½ teaspoon salt
1 teaspoon vanilla
½ cup walnuts or pecans, chopped
Chocolate Frosting (recipe below)

Preheat waffle iron, according to manufacturer's directions, and grease lightly if necessary. In a small saucepan, melt chocolate and butter or margarine. Stir, then set aside. In a medium bowl, beat eggs, then add sugar. Pour chocolate mixture into egg mixture. Add flour, salt, vanilla, and nuts, and mix well. When waffle iron is ready to use, drop tablespoons of batter onto lower half to form cookies; be sure cookies are at least ½ inch from edge. Bring cover down gently, and bake for 25 to 30 seconds, or until done. Cool, then frost with Chocolate Frosting. Makes 2 dozen cookies.

CHOCOLATE FROSTING

1 square (1 ounce) unsweetened
    chocolate
5 tablespoons butter

¼ cup milk
½ cup granulated sugar
1½ to 2 cups confectioners' sugar

In a saucepan combine chocolate, butter, milk, and granulated sugar. Stirring constantly, bring mixture to a boil; cook until sugar is dissolved. Remove from heat. Beat in confectioners' sugar until smooth. Cool, then frost cookies.

BUTTERSCOTCH SQUARES

¼ cup butter or margarine
1 cup brown sugar
1 egg
1 teaspoon vanilla
1 cup flour

¼ teaspoon salt
1 teaspoon baking powder
⅓ cup walnuts or almonds, chopped
Walnut halves or whole almonds

Cream together butter or margarine, brown sugar, egg, and vanilla. In a separate bowl, combine flour, salt, and baking powder; stir into creamed mixture. Add chopped nuts and mix well. Spread mixture into a greased 9–inch square pan. Bake at 350 degrees for about 20 minutes. Cool. Frost with favorite confectioners' sugar icing, if desired, and cut into squares. Place a walnut half or an almond in each square. Makes 1½ dozen cookies.

PUFFED WHEAT TREATS

1 cup light corn syrup
2 cups brown sugar
½ cup butter

1 cup evaporated milk
⅓ cup granulated sugar
16 cups Puffed Wheat cereal

In a heavy saucepan, combine corn syrup and brown sugar. Bring to a boil over medium heat. Add butter. Stirring constantly, bring to a boil again. Add evaporated milk and granulated sugar. Cook to soft-ball stage (240 degrees on candy thermometer). While syrup is cooking, measure cereal into a very large (at least 6 quarts) pan. Remove syrup from heat and slowly pour over cereal, tossing until coated. Press into balls. Makes 20 to 24 balls.

Contributor's comment: "Whenever our family gets together, my eighty-year-old mother (who has 13 children, 82 grandchildren, and 152 great-grandchildren) makes these treats by the dozens. They are much easier to make than popcorn balls because the corn doesn't have to be popped. This is her favorite treat for the neighborhood children who come to her home on Halloween. This recipe works just as well with popcorn, if you prefer."

BAKED CARROT PUDDING

2 cups grated carrots
½ cup butter or margarine, melted
1 cup flour
1 cup sugar
½ teaspoon salt
½ teaspoon cinnamon

½ teaspoon nutmeg
½ teaspoon allspice
½ teaspoon cloves
1 teaspoon baking soda
1 cup raisins
1 cup walnuts, chopped
Lemon Sauce (recipe below)

In a large bowl, combine grated carrots and melted butter or margarine. Stir or sift together flour, sugar, salt, cinnamon, nutmeg, allspice, cloves, and baking soda. Add to carrots; mix well. Add raisins and walnuts. Pour mixture into a greased 2–quart casserole dish. Cover and bake at 300 degrees for 45 minutes. Serve warm with Lemon Sauce. Makes 10 to 12 servings.

LEMON SAUCE

1 cup sugar
2 tablespoons cornstarch
2 cups water

2 tablespoons butter or margarine
Juice of 1 lemon
Grated rind of lemon

Combine sugar, cornstarch, and water in saucepan, and stir over medium heat until thickened. Remove from heat and add butter or margarine, lemon juice, and grated lemon rind. Serve warm.

PINEAPPLE MOUSSE

1 teaspoon unflavored gelatin	1 tablespoon lemon juice
1 tablespoon cold water	½ cup sugar
½ cup crushed pineapple with juice	1 cup whipping cream

Soften gelatin in cold water. Combine pineapple with juice, lemon juice, and sugar; add gelatin mixture. Whip cream and fold into pineapple mixture. Pour into a 1–quart mold and refrigerate for at least 4 hours. Makes 6 to 8 servings.

POMEGRANATE SALAD

4 cups pomegranate seeds	½ cup walnuts, chopped
2 apples, diced	1 cup whipping cream
2 bananas, diced	

Combine pomegranate seeds, apples, bananas, and walnuts. Refrigerate. Just before serving, whip cream and fold into fruit mixture. Makes 12 servings.

GRENADINE SYRUP

4 cups pomegranate juice	2 cups sugar

In a heavy saucepan, combine juice with sugar and stir. Heat to simmering and simmer 3 to 5 minutes. Cool. Store syrup in refrigerator for one to two weeks, or in the freezer. Use as topping for ice cream or chilled fruits or in beverages. Makes 4 cups.

POMEGRANATE SAUCE

½ cup sugar
⅛ teaspoon salt
2 tablespoons cornstarch
¾ cup boiling water

¾ cup pomegranate juice
1 tablespoon lemon juice
1 tablespoon butter or margarine

In a heavy saucepan, combine sugar, salt, and cornstarch. Stir in boiling water and pomegranate juice. Bring to a boil, stirring constantly. Boil one minute. Remove from heat, and add lemon juice and butter; mix well. Serve hot on waffles or pudding, or serve cold on ice cream, sponge cake, or angel food cake. Makes 1½ cups.

POMEGRANATE JELLY

3½ cups pomegranate juice
¼ cup lemon juice

1 package (1.75 ounces) pectin
4½ cups sugar

Combine pomegranate juice, lemon juice, and pectin in a large pot. Bring to a boil over medium high heat, stirring constantly. Stir in sugar until well blended; return to a boil and continue boiling uncovered, stirring occasionally, for 2 minutes. Remove from heat immediately. Let stand a minute to allow foam to form; then carefully skim off the foam. Pour hot jelly into hot sterilized jars, filling to within about ½ inch of tops. Carefully wipe off rim of jar. Put lid on each jar as it is filled, and screw band on tightly. Process in hot-water bath 5 minutes. Makes enough jelly to fill 6 half-pint jars.

PRICKLY PEAR JELLY

5½ cups prickly pear juice
(directions below)
¼ cup lemon juice

1 package (1.75 ounces) pectin
7½ cups sugar

In a saucepan, combine prickly pear juice and lemon juice; add pectin. Stir over medium heat until all the pectin is dissolved and no particles linger on the sides of the pan. Place over high heat and, stirring constantly, bring to a boil. Add sugar. Continuing to stir, bring to a full rolling boil, and boil hard for exactly two minutes. Remove from heat and skim off foam. Pour into sterilized jars to within ¼ inch from top. Place lids on jars, and screw bands on tightly. Process jars in hot-water bath for 10 minutes. Makes enough jelly to fill 9 or 10 half-pint jars.

PREPARING PRICKLY PEAR JUICE

To pick prickly pears, wear heavy leather gloves and long sleeves and pants. Using long-handled tongs, grasp the fruit and gently pick it. Pears are ready to harvest when the color is a dark reddish purple and pears can be removed from cactus easily, without pulling, tugging, or twisting. If pears are picked too soon, jelly made from the juice will not set up firmly; however, the thin jelly may be used as syrup for pancakes and waffles.

Place prickly pears in a colander and rinse well, being careful not to bruise fruit. Place in a heavy pan and cover with water; over medium heat bring to a boil and continue cooking until the pears are soft and mash easily, about 30 to 45 minutes. Remove from heat.

To strain the juice, use two old, clean pillowcases with a high, tight thread count. Place one pillowcase over a large container and pour the pulp and juice over it; do not force pulp through the cloth. Repeat the process, using second clean pillowcase. Store juice in refrigerator or pour into sterilized jars and seal tightly until ready to prepare jelly.

GRANOLA

8 cups rolled oats
6 cups rolled wheat
2 cups wheat germ
2 teaspoons salt
1¼ cups brown sugar
2 cups raisins

½ cup honey
1 cup water
1 cup oil
1 tablespoon vanilla
2 cups flaked coconut
1 cup nuts, chopped

Combine rolled oats, rolled wheat, wheat germ, salt, brown sugar, and raisins. Mix together honey, water, oil, and vanilla, and pour over dry ingredients. Stir to mix well. Add coconut and nuts. Spread onto four cookie sheets. Bake at 225 degrees for 2 hours. Store in airtight containers. Makes approximately 4 quarts. For variation, add sunflower seeds.

MOLASSES CANDY

1½ cups sugar
1½ cups molasses
1 cup heavy cream

3 tablespoons butter
¼ teaspoon baking soda
1 cup almonds, whole or slivered

In a heavy saucepan, bring sugar, molasses, cream, and butter to a boil. Stirring constantly, cook to hard-ball stage (265 to 270 degrees on candy thermometer). Remove from heat, and stir in baking soda and almonds. Pour onto buttered cookie sheet. When cool, break into pieces. Makes 1½ pounds.

PECAN ROLLS

3½ cups sugar
¾ cup light corn syrup
¾ cup water

3 egg whites
Caramel Coating (recipe below)
2 cups pecans, chopped

In a heavy saucepan, combine sugar, corn syrup, and water. Stirring constantly, boil until candy reaches soft-crack stage (275 degrees on candy thermometer). Remove from heat. In a large mixing bowl, beat egg whites to medium peaks. Pour hot syrup mixture into egg white slowly, and beat or stir until it sets up. On a greased surface, divide candy into 4 large pieces; roll each piece until it is about 5 inches long. Set aside while preparing Caramel Coating (recipe below). Then dip each roll of candy into caramel coating and roll in pecans. Place each piece on waxed paper or buttered cookie sheet until cool. Wrap in wax paper.

CARAMEL COATING

2 cups sugar
¼ cup flour
¼ cup cornstarch

2 cups evaporated milk
⅔ cup light corn syrup
½ cup butter or margarine

In a heavy saucepan, combine sugar, flour, cornstarch, evaporated milk, corn syrup, and butter or margarine. Bring to a boil, and cook over medium heat to firm-ball stage (248 degrees on candy thermometer, or until a small ball, dropped into cold water, holds its shape when pressed). Remove from heat and cool. Then proceed to complete Pecan Rolls as directed above.

PEANUT BUTTER FUDGE

3 cups sugar
¼ cup cocoa
2 tablespoons light corn syrup
¼ teaspoon salt

1½ cups heavy cream
2 heaping tablespoons peanut butter
2 teaspoons vanilla
1 cup chopped walnuts

In a heavy saucepan, mix sugar and cocoa. Stir in corn syrup, salt, and cream. Bring to a boil over medium heat and, stirring constantly, cook to soft-ball stage (240 degrees on candy thermometer). Pour out onto buttered marble slab or into a buttered bowl to cool. Do not scrape pan, or candy will become sugary. When cool, add peanut butter and vanilla. Beat with a wooden spatula until candy loses its gloss. Stir in nuts. If candy becomes crumbly, knead until it is smooth. Put in a 9-inch square buttered pan; when candy sets up, cut into squares. Makes 2 pounds.

DIVINITY

2⅔ cups sugar
⅔ cup light corn syrup
⅔ cup water
¼ teaspoon salt

2 egg whites
1 teaspoon vanilla
1 cup walnuts, chopped

In a heavy saucepan, combine sugar, corn syrup, water, and salt. Bring to a boil over medium heat and cook to hard-crack stage (300 degrees on candy thermometer, or small amount of syrup dropped into cold water forms a string that cracks). While syrup is cooking, beat egg whites until they form stiff peaks. Remove syrup from heat and, beating constantly with an electric mixer, gradually pour over egg whites. Continue beating until candy loses its gloss. Remove beaters, and stir in vanilla and nuts. Drop by teaspoonfuls onto wax paper or buttered pan. Makes 1½ pounds.

5 · DINOSAURLAND

Dinosaurland encompasses Utah's highest mountain range, the Uintas; several large reservoirs, popular for boating and fishing; and the intriguing quarry at Dinosaur National Monument, where the fossilized remains of over two thousand bones can be viewed. The quarry area was discovered in 1909, and by 1915 the vicinity was designated a national monument. Visitors can watch as paleontologists chip away the dirt and expose the fossilized bones. In nearby Vernal, Dinosaur Gardens has fourteen life-sized dinosaur reproductions, and the Utah Field House of Natural History offers explanations of the prehistoric past.

This region has a very old story to tell. The Uinta Basin is the geographical remains of the prehistoric Uinta Lake, formed in the Tertiary period. Indian remains also provide evidence of peoples from prehistoric times and, beginning in about A.D. 1000, the Fremont Indians. In more recent times, the Utes began inhabiting the area. In 1861, the same year a search party sent to the region described it as a "vast contiguity of waste and measurable valueless land," President Abraham Lincoln created the Uintah Indian Reservation, to which many tribes were forced to migrate. In 1888, gilsonite was discovered and the federal government withdrew seven thousand acres from the reservation for mining.

In 1887 the Dawes Severalty Act provided for land on Indian reservations to be allotted to individual tribe members and then opened up the remaining land to homesteaders. Over the next few years settlers began to immigrate to the Uinta Basin. As a result, settlement of the area is unique in Utah history. It came from individuals who obtained their 160 acres through the Homestead Act rather than from colonists sent by Mormon leaders. This led to a somewhat more diverse group of residents in the northeastern part of the state; among them were Butch Cassidy and the Wild Bunch, who knew the hidden canyons better than anyone.

In some ways, this region has not changed much in recent years, for agriculture and livestock still form the basis of the economy. But today rich deposits of oil and natural gas have brought some industry. Tourism has also brought many visitors, drawn not only to the dinosaur remains but also to mountains and forests, crystal-clear natural lakes and man-made reservoirs, trout fishing and whitewater rafting. The natural beauties of the region are enhanced each spring and summer when more than two hundred varieties of wildflowers dot the hills and valleys.

Three counties make up Dinosaurland, each with its own unique features. Daggett County, which borders Wyoming and Colorado in the northeastern part of the region, boasts such popular attractions as Flaming Gorge, a reservoir straddling the Utah-Wyoming border on the Green River. Uintah County is home to the dinosaur quarry and the western section of Dinosaur National Monument, which sprawls across eastern Utah into Colorado. Duchesne County's natural attractions include most of the million-acre Ashley National Forest in the Uintas, the western hemisphere's largest east-west mountain range. Within these mountains are more than two dozen peaks over 13,000 feet, including King's Peak, at 13,528 feet the state's highest peak.

Dinosaurland has rich resources of food supply. On the Uintah and Ouray Indian reservations, Native Americans dry corn in the same way as their ancestors did. Abundant supplies of fish are found in the lakes and streams. The Green River below Flaming Gorge Dam has been called "one of the best trout fishing rivers in the world." Hunting season in the fall provides deer, elk, and other wild game, which are prepared in a variety of ways, from simple broiling over a fire to dried meat, roasts, and stews. All of these resources are as important today as they were to the early tribes and settlers.

Fruit and honey are other specialties found here. Chokecherries, which grow wild along the roadsides, make deliciously tart syrups, jams, and jellies. Fruits, especially apples, are enjoyed in pies, cakes, cobblers, muffins, and other favorite dishes. Honey has been an important product in Vernal, the county seat of Uintah County, since the nineteenth century when a local family brought beehives in from Idaho and opened a honey business. Honey Nut Bars became their favorite treat.

These are just a few reminders of the past in an area where time seems to have moved more slowly than in Utah's other regions. The fossilized bones of ancient giant creatures remain as reminders of the past. Modern tribal groups still live on lands first explored by their ancestors. And the widely scattered small towns are still surrounded by ranches and vast tracts of undisturbed lands, giving the region a unique lifestyle.

OUTLAW TRAIL POT ROAST AND VEGETABLES

½ cup shortening
4 to 5 pounds boneless beef roast
6 to 8 medium red potatoes, cut into chunks about 1½ inches in diameter
6 to 8 medium carrots, cut into bite-size chunks

2 onions, diced
2 celery ribs, diced
4 cups canned tomatoes with juice
3 to 4 cans (8 ounces each) tomato sauce
Salt and pepper to taste
Garlic salt to taste

In a 16- or 18-inch Dutch oven over an open fire, melt shortening until it sizzles when a few drops of water are sprinkled on pan. Cut roast into 4 or 5 pieces, and add to hot shortening. Brown well on all sides. Add vegetables, placing carrots on the bottom, then potatoes, then mixture of onions and celery. Pour tomatoes, including juice, and tomato sauce over vegetables and meat, mashing tomatoes down with the back of a large spoon. Add salt, pepper, and garlic salt to taste. Leave at least one inch of space at the top of the Dutch oven. Cover and heat until vegetables are boiling.

Set covered Dutch oven in a hole with hot coals in the bottom. Place hot coals over the lid and around the sides. Bury pot with dirt, leaving the tip of the handle sticking out of the dirt. Pack dirt firmly with the back of a shovel. Leave in ground to 4 to 8 hours. (Pot roast and vegetables should be tender in about 4 hours but can be left up to 8 hours without overcooking.) Remove Dutch oven carefully from ground, being careful not to disturb the lid so dirt will not fall into food. Remove roast from Dutch oven and slice. Serve with vegetables. Makes 8 to 10 servings.

Contributor's comment: "This recipe illustrates the original purpose of the Dutch oven, allowing the food to cook but not become overcooked. A cowboy could prepare his food early in the day and bury his Dutch oven, leave to do a day's work, and return to a hot meal. A hardtack (biscuit) completed the meal, making it hard to beat!"

Hotel Utah Borscht (p. 145); Watercress Salad (p. 147); Henefer's Heavenly Rolls (p. 173).

Clockwise from top left: Dixie Pecan Pie (p. 80); Mary's Cherry Pie (p. 45); Festival Peach Pie (p. 133); Cache Valley Cheesecake (p. 15) with Raspberry Sauce (p. 23); Bertha's Raisin Cream Pie (p. 175).

HONEY MUSTARD STEAKS

4 boneless top loin or rib eye steaks,
  cut 1 inch thick
1½ tablespoons honey
⅓ cup prepared mustard
1 tablespoon chopped parsley

1 tablespoon vinegar
1 tablespoon water
¼ teaspoon hot pepper sauce
⅛ teaspoon black pepper

In a small bowl, combine honey, mustard, parsley, vinegar, water, pepper sauce, and black pepper. Grill steaks over medium coals, brushing with honey mustard glaze and turning once.

HONEY-LIME BEEF

1 sirloin steak (about 2 pounds), cut
  1 inch thick
1 can (11 ounces) beef broth
2 tablespoons brown sugar
1 tablespoon honey

¼ cup soy sauce
3 tablespoons lime juice
¼ cup chopped green onions
1 garlic clove, crushed

In a mixing bowl combine beef broth, brown sugar, honey, soy sauce, lime juice, green onions, and garlic. Mix well. Pour over steak, turning to coat both sides of meat, and marinate in refrigerator at least 4 hours. Grill to desired doneness, brushing once or twice with marinade. Makes 4 to 6 servings.

SOUR CREAM CHICKEN BREASTS

6 chicken breasts, boned and
   skinned
1 cup sour cream
2 tablespoons lemon juice
½ teaspoon salt

1 teaspoon seasoning salt
1 teaspoon paprika
Garlic salt or garlic powder to taste
½ cup butter or margarine
1½ cups fine bread crumbs

In a mixing bowl, combine sour cream with lemon juice, salt, seasoning salt, paprika, and garlic salt or garlic powder to taste. Dip chicken breasts in sour cream mixture and place in a buttered 9 x 13–inch baking dish. In a saucepan, melt butter or margarine and add bread crumbs, stirring with a fork just until crumbs are coated. Sprinkle coated bread crumbs on top of chicken. Cover and bake at 325 degrees until chicken is tender, about 1 hour. Remove cover and continue to bake for 15 to 20 minutes. Makes 6 servings.

VENISON PARMESAN

6 venison steaks, cut ½–inch thick
Salt and pepper to taste
2 eggs, beaten
2 cups bread crumbs
Cooking oil
2 cans (8 ounces each) tomato sauce

¼ teaspoon garlic powder
¼ teaspoon basil
¼ teaspoon oregano
½ teaspoon parsley
1½ cups grated Parmesan or
   mozzarella cheese

Pound steaks to tenderize. Season with salt and pepper. Dip steak in beaten egg and then bread crumbs to coat well. Heat a small amount of oil over medium-high heat; fry steaks until nearly done (if they brown too fast, lower heat). Remove from frying pan and place, in one layer, in a glass baking dish. In a mixing bowl, combine tomato sauce, garlic powder, basil, oregano, and parsley. Mix well. Spoon over steaks. Cover and bake at 350 degrees for 30 minutes. Remove from oven, and sprinkle over each steak ¼ cup cheese. Return to oven and bake, uncovered, 10 minutes.

BEEF AND BARLEY SOUP

3 to 4 pounds meaty beef shanks or
    elk neck bones
1 large onion, diced
1 cup diced celery
1 can (14½ ounces) stewed tomatoes

2½ quarts water
1½ teaspoons salt
½ teaspoon pepper
½ cup pearl barley
1½ cups diced carrots

In a large soup kettle, brown meat in its own fat over medium heat. Remove meat and set aside. Add onion and celery to drippings in kettle. Sauté until onion is tender. Add tomatoes, water, salt, pepper, and meat; bring to a boil. Reduce heat and simmer until meat is tender. Remove meat, and trim and discard fat and bones. Return meat to soup; add barley and carrots. Simmer, uncovered, for 50 minutes or until barley is soft. Makes 6 servings.

RED AND GREEN CHILI

1 pound lean ground beef
1 large onion, chopped
1 tablespoon oil
2 cups stewed tomatoes, diced
3 cups spicy tomato juice
1 can (16 ounces) pinto beans,
    undrained
1 can (16 ounces) black beans,
    undrained

1 can (16 ounces) kidney beans,
    undrained
1 can (16 ounces) refried beans
1 can (8 ounces) green chilies
½ teaspoon salt
¼ teaspoon garlic powder
½ teaspoon celery salt
Jalapeños to taste (optional)

In a heavy pot over medium heat, brown ground beef and onions in oil. Drain off excess fat. Add remaining ingredients. Mix well. Simmer for at least 45 minutes. Makes 8 to 10 servings.

JOSIE'S BARBECUE SAUCE

¼ cup oil or butter
1 cup diced onion
½ cup diced green pepper
2 garlic cloves, minced
1 tablespoon dry mustard

2 cups catsup
2 cups chili sauce
½ cup honey
½ cup brown sugar
Liquid smoke (optional)

In a large, heavy skillet, heat oil or butter. Add onions, green peppers, garlic, and mustard, and sauté until vegetables are tender. Stir in catsup, chili sauce, honey, brown sugar, and, if desired, a few drops liquid smoke. Simmer for 30 minutes. Store in refrigerator.

HONEY BAKED BEANS

1 pound ground pork sausage
1 large onion, diced
1 large green pepper, diced
½ cup barbecue sauce
½ cup catsup
½ cup honey

½ cup brown sugar
2 tablespoons Worcestershire sauce
1 can (8 ounces) pineapple tidbits
4 cans (16 ounces each) pork and
  beans

In a large skillet, brown sausage. Add onion and green pepper, and sauté until vegetables are tender. Add barbecue sauce, catsup, honey, brown sugar, Worcestershire sauce, and pineapple. Mix well. Stir in beans, and pour into a 4–quart casserole dish. Bake, uncovered, at 350 degrees for 1½ hours.

GRANDMA LYMAN'S 1870s-STYLE BEANS

2 cups Great Northern or pinto
    beans
2 quarts water
1 cup chopped onion
½ cup molasses

¼ cup brown sugar
1 teaspoon dry mustard
1 teaspoon salt
4 slices salt pork
6 to 8 slices bacon

Sort and rinse beans. In a heavy pot, place beans and water. Cover and soak overnight. Do not drain. Bring beans and onion to a boil in soaking water; cover pan and cook until beans are tender, about 1 to 1½ hours. Remove from heat and drain, reserving liquid. In a large mixing bowl, combine 1 cup of the reserved liquid, molasses, brown sugar, dry mustard, and salt. Add beans. Put salt pork in bottom of a baking pan. Pour bean mixture over salt pork and cover pan. Bake at 300 degrees for 3 hours. Check periodically; if beans become dry, add more of the reserved liquid. While beans are baking, cut bacon slices in half and fry. Drain and set aside. When beans have cooked for 3 hours, remove from oven and place bacon slices on top. Cover pan and return to oven; bake an additional 45 minutes. Makes 6 to 8 servings.

BUTCH'S WILD BUNCH BREAKFAST

1 to 2 pounds spicy-hot pork sausage
    links, cut up
½ pound bacon, cut up
1 medium onion, diced

7 pounds potatoes, peeled and sliced
1 small can diced jalapeños
15 eggs, beaten
1 pound grated cheddar cheese

In a 12- to 14-inch Dutch oven, brown sausage, bacon, and onions. Drain off fat, and set aside 1 cup of the meat. Add potato slices, and cook about 45 minutes. Stir jalapeños into eggs, and pour over potatoes. Cover pan and put onto fire, placing about 10 briquettes on top. Cook for 15 minutes. Remove from fire and add cheese and reserved meat mixture. Let set for 5 minutes. Makes 12 generous servings.

QUEEN ANN'S PICKLED EGGS

2 cups juice from pickled beets
½ cup vinegar
¼ teaspoon salt

¼ cup sugar
1 teaspoon pickling spice
6 eggs

Put pickle juice in saucepan and add enough water to make 2½ cups. Stirring over medium heat, add vinegar, salt, sugar, and pickling spice. Bring to a boil, then remove from heat. Set aside. Place eggs in saucepan and add cold water to cover 1 inch above eggs. Bring water to boil over medium heat. Cover pan and remove from heat; let stand 20 minutes. Plunge eggs in cold water; then crack and peel. Place eggs in a bowl; cover with beet juice, and refrigerate 24 hours before serving.

PIONEER SODA BREAD

3 cups flour
2 tablespoons sugar
2 teaspoons baking powder
½ teaspoon baking soda

1½ cups raisins or currants (or a
    combination of the two)
1½ cups buttermilk
½ teaspoon salt

Combine all ingredients in a large bowl; stir until a soft dough forms. Turn dough onto a floured surface, and knead just until it makes a smooth ball. Form dough into a dome shape. Make a cross on top with a sharp knife. Place on a greased baking pan, and bake at 350 degrees for 45 minutes.

Note: Bread may also be baked in a Dutch oven, using 9 briquettes on the bottom and 15 on the top of a 12-inch oven.

JOY'S BUTTER ROLLS

2 cups milk
6 tablespoons sugar
¼ cup butter or margarine
3 packages (1 tablespoon each)
  active dry yeast

½ cup warm water
3 eggs, beaten
6 cups flour
1 teaspoon salt
½ cup butter or margarine

In a heavy saucepan, scald milk. Add sugar and ¼ cup butter or margarine; stir until sugar is dissolved and butter or margarine is melted. Remove from heat. In a small cup or bowl, dissolve yeast in warm water. In a large bowl, beat eggs. Combine milk, yeast, and eggs. Mix well. Add flour and salt. Mix, adding more flour if needed, until a soft dough forms. Knead dough several times. Place dough in greased bowl, turning once to coat top. Cover with a clean dish towel, and let rise until double in bulk. Melt ½ cup butter or margarine in a 9 x 13–inch pan. Punch dough down and pull off pieces, shaping them into rolls. Place in buttered pan, turning once to butter tops. Let rise again. Bake at 350 degrees for 30 to 35 minutes, until golden brown.

STATE FAIR MUFFINS

2 cups flour
4 teaspoons baking powder
½ teaspoon salt
1 cup milk
1 egg, well beaten

¼ cup melted shortening
½ cup raisins (optional)
2 tablespoons ground nuts
  (optional)

In a bowl, combine flour, baking powder, and salt. Set aside. In a separate bowl, combine milk, beaten egg, and melted shortening. Pour milk into flour mixture. Mix well. (The batter will be stiff.) Add raisins or nuts, if desired. Spoon batter into greased muffin tins. Bake at 350 degrees for 18 to 20 minutes. Makes 1 dozen.

Contributor's comment: "This muffin recipe is the one I used when, as a member of a 4-H cooking class, I won first place in the 1931 Utah State Fair."

SOURDOUGH BISCUITS

½ cup Clara's Sourdough Starter
   (recipe below)
1 cup milk
2½ cups sifted flour
1 tablespoon sugar
¾ teaspoon salt

1¼ teaspoons baking powder
½ teaspoon baking soda
2 tablespoons yellow cornmeal
3 tablespoons butter or margarine
2 tablespoons oil

Night before: Put ½ cup starter in a large mixing bowl. Add milk and 1 cup of the flour. Mix well. Cover and let stand overnight in warm place.

Next day: Add 1 cup flour to starter mixture prepared the night before. Mix well. Add sugar, salt, baking powder, baking soda, and remaining ½ cup flour. Stir until dough is stiff. On lightly floured surface, knead dough about 15 times, until it is soft. Cover dough with inverted bowl and let rest for 10 minutes. Roll dough ½ inch thick and, with a lightly floured cutter, cut out biscuits. Sprinkle 1 tablespoon cornmeal on the bottom of a 13 x 9–inch baking pan. Melt butter or margarine and add oil. Dip biscuits in combined oil and arrange close together in baking pan. Sprinkle tops of biscuits with remaining 1 tablespoon cornmeal. Let rise until doubled in bulk. Bake at 375 degrees for 12 to 15 minutes, until golden brown. Makes 2 dozen biscuits.

CLARA'S SOURDOUGH STARTER

1 package (1 tablespoon) active dry
   yeast

2 cups flour
2 cups water

In a bowl mix yeast, flour, and water. Stir well. Keep in a warm place overnight. The next day, put starter into glass container with a tight lid; store, tightly covered, in refrigerator. Starter may be used in pancakes, muffins, bread, or cake. Each time starter is removed from glass container, replenish it by adding equal amounts of flour and water (½ to 1 cup flour and ½ to 1 cup water). As long as at least 1 cup starter remains when flour and water are added, yeast will remain activated.

APPLE CAKE

½ cup butter
2 cups granulated sugar
2 eggs
2 cups flour
1 teaspoon salt
1 teaspoon nutmeg

1 teaspoon cinnamon
1 teaspoon baking soda
6 apples, peeled and grated or finely chopped
½ cup brown sugar
1 cup nuts, chopped

In a large mixing bowl, cream together butter, granulated sugar, and eggs. Stir or sift together flour, salt, nutmeg, cinnamon, and baking soda; add to creamed mixture, stirring well. Add apples. Pour into a greased 9 x 13–inch baking pan. Sprinkle top with brown sugar and nuts. Bake at 350 degrees for 45 to 50 minutes. Serve hot or cold with sweetened whipped cream or vanilla sauce.

APPLE ALICE

3 apples, peeled and sliced
1 teaspoon cinnamon
1 cup sugar
1 cup flour

½ teaspoon salt
½ cup butter or margarine
1 egg

Place apples in a 9-inch glass pie plate. Combine cinnamon and sugar, and sprinkle about half over apples. In a mixing bowl combine flour and salt; cut in butter. Add egg and mix lightly. With buttered fingers, spread carefully over tops of apples (they may not be completely covered). Sprinkle with remaining sugar and cinnamon. Bake at 375 degrees until apples are done and top is golden brown, approximately 40 minutes.

Contributor's comment: "This recipe was named for my sister, who gave it to me. The difference between this cobbler and others is addition of the egg. This recipe can be used with other fruits, such as peaches or berries, but apples are the best. Apple Alice can be served warm or cold, and is delicious plain or with ice cream. We also enjoy leftover cobbler for breakfast."

COUNTRY PEACH COBBLER

2 quarts bottled or canned peaches,
   slices or halves
Cinnamon
1 cup sugar
3 cups flour

4 teaspoons baking powder
¼ cup butter or margarine
1 cup milk
3 teaspoons vanilla

Pour peaches, including juice, into a 9 x 13–inch baking dish and sprinkle generously with cinnamon. (If additional sweetening is desired, sprinkle a little sugar over peaches.) In a mixing bowl, combine sugar, flour, and baking powder. Cut in butter. Add milk and vanilla, and mix well. Drop spoonfuls of dough on top of the peach mixture and sprinkle a little more cinnamon on top. Bake at 350 degrees for 40 to 45 minutes, until dough is done. Serve hot or cold, topped with milk or vanilla ice cream. Makes 8 to 10 servings. *Note:* Cobbler may be cooked in a 12– or 14–inch Dutch oven. Use 9 briquettes on the bottom and 15 on top.

SUGAR PUMPKIN-APPLE DESSERT

1 small pumpkin
8 to 12 apples, peeled and sliced
⅓ cup granulated sugar
⅓ cup brown sugar
½ teaspoon nutmeg

½ teaspoon cinnamon
1 cup raisins
1 cup walnuts, chopped
¼ cup butter or margarine

Cut top off pumpkin and remove seeds. Rub soft butter in pumpkin shell. Peel and slice apples. Set aside. Combine granulated and brown sugars, nutmeg, cinnamon, raisins, and nuts. Stir in apple slices. Place in hollowed-out pumpkin, and dot with butter. Replace top of pumpkin. Place pumpkin in baking pan in about ½ inch water. Bake at 350 degrees for about 2 hours, checking occasionally to replenish water in pan, if necessary. Dessert is done when pumpkin flesh inside the shell is cooked but not mushy. Scoop apple mixture and pumpkin into serving dishes. Top with sweetened whipped cream or ice cream, if desired. Makes 6 to 8 servings.

BUTTERMILK SUGAR COOKIES

4 cups flour
2 cups sugar
1 teaspoon salt
1 teaspoon baking soda
1 teaspoon baking powder

1 cup butter or margarine
1 egg, beaten
¾ teaspoon lemon extract
¾ cup buttermilk

In a large mixing bowl, combine flour, sugar, salt, baking soda, and baking powder; cut in butter or margarine. Add egg, lemon extract, and buttermilk. Mix well. Add more flour if necessary to make a soft dough. Cover and chill in refrigerator 60 minutes. On a floured board, roll out dough and cut into desired shapes. Place on lightly greased cookie sheet and bake at 375 degrees for 10 to 12 minutes. Makes 5 dozen.

HONEY PEANUT-BUTTER COOKIES

¼ cup shortening
½ cup peanut butter
½ cup sugar
½ cup honey
1 egg, beaten

2 cups flour
1 teaspoon baking powder
¼ teaspoon baking soda
½ teaspoon salt
¾ cup nuts, chopped

In a large mixing bowl, cream shortening and peanut butter together. Add sugar and continue creaming. Add honey gradually and beat until light. Add egg and mix well. Stir or sift together flour, baking powder, baking soda, and salt; add to creamed mixture. Stir in nuts; mix well. Form dough into 2 rolls. Wrap in wax paper and chill. Cut dough in ½–inch slices, and place on ungreased cookie sheet. Bake at 400 degrees for 6 to 8 minutes. Makes 2 dozen cookies.

Note: Cookies may also be formed by shaping dough into balls, placing them on cookie sheet, and flattening with a fork to make a crisscross pattern.

HONEY NUT BARS

½ cup shortening or margarine
½ cup sugar
½ cup honey
½ teaspoon vanilla
2 eggs, beaten
1¾ cups flour

1 teaspoon baking powder
½ teaspoon baking soda
½ teaspoon salt
1 cup rolled oats
1 cup coconut
½ cup nuts, chopped

In a large mixing bowl, cream shortening or margarine, sugar, honey, vanilla, and beaten eggs. Stir or sift together flour, baking powder, baking soda, and salt; add to creamed mixture. Mix well. Stir in oats, coconut, and nuts. Spread dough on greased 9 x 13–inch pan. Bake at 350 degrees for no longer than 12 to 14 minutes. Remove from oven when batter is barely cooked; it will continue cooking for a minute or two, and can become too dry if overcooked. Cool and cut into bars. Makes 2 dozen bars.

ALTA'S RHUBARB SPECIAL

5 cups rhubarb, cut in 1–inch pieces
1½ cups sugar
1 cup water
½ cup rolled oats

1 cup raisins
Sour cream
Chopped nuts (optional)

In a heavy saucepan combine rhubarb, sugar, water, oats, and raisins. Bring to a boil, then reduce heat and simmer, covered, for 10 minutes. Serve hot or cold with a dollop of sour cream on each serving. Top with chopped nuts, if desired. Makes 4 to 6 servings.

CHOKECHERRY JUICE AND SYRUP

Chokecherry Juice: Wash and stem 2 quarts fresh chokecherries. Put fruit in a large pot. Crush fruit and add 5 cups water. Bring to a boil. Reduce heat and simmer uncovered for 20 minutes. Remove from heat and strain to extract juice.

Chokecherry Syrup: Bring 3 cups chokecherry juice to boil. Add 7 cups sugar and bring to boil again. Boil until syrup drops are heavy and mixture shows slight "sheeting" when dropped from spoon. Pour syrup into hot, sterile jars to within ½ inch of top. Wipe top of jar with damp clean cloth. Put hot lid on and screw band tight. Cool. Test for seal after 12 hours. Makes 3 pints.

Contributor's comment: "Chokecherries, a wild fruit, are plentiful in our area. Chokecherry jelly can be made by cooking the syrup longer or adding pectin."

6 · GOLDEN SPIKE EMPIRE

The Golden Spike Empire encompasses over eight thousand square miles in northwestern Utah—from the Wasatch Mountains to the east, through the Great Salt Lake, and to the Great Basin on the west. The topography ranges from high mountains to salt desert, large bodies of water, rich farmlands, and extensive marshlands. Antelope Island State Park, an island in the Great Salt Lake, has six hundred bison roaming over its twenty-three thousand acres.

One of the most famous sites, the one that gives the region its name, is the Golden Spike National Historic site at Promontory, near the northern end of the lake. On May 10, 1869, the Central Pacific Railroad met the Union Pacific Railroad there and a golden spike was driven, marking completion of the first transcontinental railway line.

The history of the region is similar to that of the surrounding area. Prehistoric hunters and gatherers roamed the land as early as twelve thousand years ago. In more recent times, the Shoshoni and the Utes hunted and fished in the foothills of today's Weber County. Mountain men came in the early 1800s, led by Jim Bridger, the first white man to report sighting the Great Salt Lake. The first white settlement was established in 1841 when trapper Miles Goodyear established a trading post and fort on the banks of the Weber River. In 1847 the Mormon pioneers, led by Brigham Young, began arriving in the Salt Lake Valley, and by 1850 more than a thousand pioneer colonists had moved thirty-five miles north to Goodyear's area. The town they established, Ogden, was named after Peter Skene Ogden, a fur trapper for the Hudson Bay Company who explored nearby but never actually set foot on the site.

Soon after completion of the transcontinental railroad, the main junction was moved to Ogden, which became known as the "Junction City." With the railroad came many new industries. One of them, firearms, resulted when local inventor John Browning patented a new single-shot rifle in 1879.

The next population boom came during World War II. Several military installations, including Defense Depot Ogden, the Ogden Arsenal, Hill Air Force Base, the Naval Supply Depot, and Bushnell General Army Hospital were built within a few miles of Ogden. These installations brought many jobs and people; in the early 1940s, as many as 150 trains a day stopped in Ogden. Some of the facilities were dismantled after the war, but others continue to serve the nation's military needs.

As in the past, the region still has many farms, orchards, and ranches, but major industries and businesses have also been established. Minuteman Missiles and space-shuttle booster rockets, jet engines and Jetway loading bridges are manufactured in the region, which also is home to the Internal Revenue Service's Ogden processing center, U.S. Forest Service operations, and Weber State University.

Outdoor activities draw many thousands each year to Golden Spike Empire's mountains, lakes, streams, wetlands, and historic sites. Bordering the region on the east are the rugged Wasatch Mountains and the Cache National Forest, and on the west, the Great Salt Lake and desert lands. Willard Bay State Park, popular with boaters, is a 10,000–acre freshwater bay on the flood plain of the Great Salt Lake. Hundreds of species of birds may be observed at three large wetland areas: the Ogden Bay and Farmington Bay Waterfowl Management areas and the Bear River Migratory Bird Refuge.

Interesting historic sites include restored buildings along Ogden's 25th Street, a reminder of the city's colorful railroad past; Union Station, site of the John M. Browning Firearms Museum and the Railroad Museum; and Fort Buenaventura, a stockade replica built on the site of Miles Goodyear's fort. The area's Mormon heritage is represented by the Box Elder LDS Tabernacle in Brigham City, built in 1881, and the Farmington Rock Chapel, built in 1862–63. Other faiths are represented by the Methodist Church in Corinne, built in 1870 and believed to be the first non-Mormon church in Utah, and a Trappist Monastery in Huntsville that was established in 1947.

Agricultural products of the Golden Spike Empire are celebrated in such local community festivals as Tomato Days, Beet Days, Peach Days, and county fairs. Numerous produce stands along Utah's famous "Fruitway" on U.S. 89 south of Brigham City attract residents and tourists to the fruits and vegetables harvested in the region, from strawberries and peas in early summer to pumpkins in late fall. Favorite recipes from the area's good cooks take advantage of the locally grown produce in such dishes as Parsnips with Brown Butter, Sweet Pickled Beets, Holiday Carrots, Rhubarb Crunch, Chocolate Potato Cake, Apricot Cake, and peach pie, tarts, and ice cream.

MITCH'S BUFFALO BARBECUE

2 pounds buffalo roast or steak,
    cooked and sliced into thin strips
1 medium onion, diced
1 medium green pepper, diced
1 cup fresh mushrooms, diced
1 clove garlic, minced, or 1½
    teaspoons garlic powder
1 tablespoon chili powder

Salt and pepper to taste
¼ to ½ cup water
1 can (8 ounces) tomato sauce
1 tablespoon prepared mustard
1 tablespoon Worcestershire sauce
Cayenne pepper sauce
¼ cup honey, or to taste

In a large, heavy pan, combine buffalo meat, onion, green pepper, mushrooms, garlic, chili powder, salt, pepper, and water. Cook over low heat until vegetables are tender. Mix together tomato sauce, mustard, Worcestershire sauce, 3 to 4 dashes cayenne pepper sauce, and honey; add to the meat mixture. Simmer for 20 minutes. Serve on buns. Makes 10 to 12 servings.

Contributor's comment: "Antelope Island on the Great Salt Lake is the home of a large herd of bison (they are not true buffalo). Introduced to the island in 1893, they were left to roam on their own for nearly a century. In 1987 the Utah Division of Wildlife Resources began the first herd management practices, and three years later a new bloodline was introduced into the original herd. The herd's 'bisontennial' was celebrated in 1993. Today bison can be seen in their natural habitat on the island. Buffalo, of the same genus as bison, is one of the healthiest meats available, with more protein and less fat and calories than other red meats, chicken, or fish."

PRIZE-WINNING BARBECUED PORK RIBS

2 tablespoons butter
2 tablespoons diced green pepper
½ cup diced onions
¼ cup diced celery
2 garlic cloves, minced
2 tablespoons lemon juice
1 cup brown sugar
2 tablespoons vinegar
2 teaspoons Worcestershire sauce
5 teaspoons taco sauce
1 teaspoon horseradish

1 cup catsup
½ cup prepared mustard
1 can (8 ounces) tomato sauce
½ can (6 ounces) tomato paste
1 teaspoon lemon pepper
1 teaspoon dry mustard
1 teaspoon garlic salt
3 drops liquid smoke
4 racks of pork ribs
Salt and pepper to taste

At least four hours before cooking meat, prepare barbecue sauce: In a large, heavy saucepan, melt butter. Add green pepper, onions, celery, and garlic, and sauté until vegetables are tender, about 2 to 3 minutes. Add lemon juice and simmer slowly for 15 minutes. Add brown sugar, vinegar, Worcestershire sauce, taco sauce, horseradish, catsup, prepared mustard, tomato sauce, tomato paste, lemon pepper, dry mustard, garlic salt, and liquid smoke. Mix well. Simmer slowly, stirring occasionally, for about 3 hours.

Place ribs on heated grill. Cook on both sides, basting occasionally with barbecue sauce, until ribs reach desired degree of doneness. Makes 8 to 10 servings.

CHICKEN AND ASPARAGUS CASSEROLE

1 large chicken (3 to 4 pounds)	1 teaspoon salt
2 cups fresh asparagus, steamed	¼ teaspoon pepper
3 cups bread crumbs	1 cup chicken broth
¾ cup butter, melted	2 cups milk
¼ cup butter	2 cups cheddar cheese, shredded
½ cup flour	

At least two hours in advance, prepare chicken: Wash and dry chicken. Place in large pot and add just enough cold water to cover; add salt to taste. Bring to a boil and skim off foam. Cover pan, and simmer until chicken is tender. Remove from heat. Strain (reserving broth), and remove skin and bones. Cut meat into bite-size pieces. Refrigerate until ready to use.

Steam asparagus until tender crisp. Drain and set aside. In a mixing bowl, combine bread crumbs and ¾ cup melted butter. Set aside. In a heavy saucepan over medium heat, melt ¼ cup butter. Add flour, salt, and pepper, and mix until smooth. Slowly add chicken broth and milk; cook, stirring constantly, until sauce comes to a boil and is thickened. Stir in chicken.

In a 9 x 13–inch casserole dish, spread half of the buttered crumbs. Place asparagus spears on top of crumbs. Cover with creamed chicken mixture. Sprinkle rest of crumbs on top of casserole. Bake, uncovered, at 350 degrees for 25 minutes. Sprinkle with cheese, and bake for additional 5 minutes. Makes 6 to 8 servings.

Note: 3 cups cooked, diced turkey may be used in place of chicken.

Contributor's comment: "In the spring of 1859, a Mr. Rollett brought asparagus plant seeds to Plain City, Utah, from France. He soon discovered that the soil and climate provided the right conditions for the spring vegetable. Soon several families were planting small patches of asparagus and selling it to grocery stores and fruit and vegetable peddlers in Ogden. Today asparagus is grown in several large open fields."

COUNTRY FRIED CHICKEN

2 broiler-fryer chickens (about 3 to 4
    pounds each), cut up
1 quart buttermilk
2 cups flour

1 tablespoon paprika
1½ teaspoons salt
1½ teaspoons fresh ground pepper
Cooking oil

Marinate chicken pieces in buttermilk for 8 hours. Combine flour, paprika, salt, and pepper. Coat chicken pieces evenly in flour mixture. In a large, heavy skillet, pour oil ½-inch deep; heat. Place chicken, skin side down, in skillet. (Put larger, meatier pieces in first.) Fry, uncovered, in hot oil for 15 to 25 minutes on each side, turning only once. Drain well on absorbent paper. Makes 8 servings.

PLAIN CITY SAGE DRESSING

1 large loaf of bread, broken in
    pieces
1 teaspoon baking powder
Sage to taste
1 cup diced onions

1 cup diced celery
4 eggs, beaten
1⅓ cups butter, melted
Salt and pepper to taste
Milk

In a large bowl combine bread, baking powder, and sage. Add onion, celery, eggs, melted butter, and salt and pepper. Stir in just enough milk to moisten. Spoon into a greased 9 x 9-inch baking dish. Dot with butter. Bake at 350 degrees for 40 minutes. Makes 6 to 8 servings.

EDNA'S CHICKEN NOODLE SOUP

1 stewing hen (4 to 5 pounds)
2 quarts water
2 teaspoons salt
¼ teaspoon pepper
2 chicken bouillon cubes
½ cup diced carrots

½ cup diced celery
½ cup diced onion
1 tablespoon chopped fresh parsley
Edna's Homemade Noodles (recipe
  below)

Put chicken in a large kettle and cover with cold water. Add salt and pepper. Bring to a boil and skim off foam. Cover pan and simmer for 2½ hours or until meat falls off the bone. Remove chicken; discard skin and bones. Cool broth slightly, and skim off the fat that rises to the top. Cut chicken into pieces and return to broth. Bring broth to a boil and add chicken bouillon, carrots, celery, and onion. Simmer for ten minutes; then increase heat until soup is boiling. Add Edna's Homemade Noodles and boil until noodles rise to the surface and are tender, about 3 to 5 minutes. Sprinkle with parsley and serve piping hot. Makes 6 to 8 servings.

EDNA'S HOMEMADE NOODLES

1 cup flour
½ teaspoon salt

2 large eggs
¼ cup half-and-half

Combine flour and salt in a bowl. Make well in center and add eggs and half-and-half. Stir with fork until well mixed. Form into a ball and turn out on lightly floured surface. Knead 15 minutes, adding flour if needed to make a soft dough. Cover and let rest 10 minutes. Divide dough into two portions, covering one portion until other portion has been rolled out. Roll out each portion until paper thin. Dust top with flour and fold dough over. With a sharp knife, cut into strips about ½ inch wide and 2 to 3 inches long. Separate noodles and add to chicken soup as directed above.

GRANDMOTHER STOKER'S BAKED BEANS

10 slices bacon, cut into pieces
½ pound ground beef
½ cup chopped onions
⅓ cup granulated sugar
⅓ cup brown sugar
2 tablespoons molasses
¼ cup barbecue sauce
¼ cup catsup
2 tablespoons prepared mustard
½ teaspoon salt
½ teaspoon pepper
½ teaspoon garlic powder
1 cup crushed pineapple and juice
1 can (16 ounces) kidney beans, drained
1 can (16 ounces) pork and beans
1 can (16 ounces) butter beans

In a large skillet, brown bacon, ground beef, and onions. Drain excess fat. Add rest of ingredients and mix well. Pour into a 3–quart casserole dish. Bake, uncovered, at 350 degrees for 1 hour. Makes 8 to 10 servings.

RED BEANS AND RICE

2 pounds spicy pork sausage
2 large onions, chopped
½ green pepper, chopped
3 cans (16 ounces each) red beans
1 teaspoon garlic salt
2 tablespoons chili sauce
1 teaspoon Worcestershire sauce
Tabasco sauce to taste
Hot steamed rice

In a heavy skillet, sauté sausage, onions, and green pepper until lightly brown. Add beans, garlic salt, chili sauce, Worcestershire sauce, and Tabasco sauce, and simmer for 1 hour. Serve over hot steamed rice. Makes 6 servings.

JULIE'S FAVORITE POTATOES

6 medium potatoes　　　　　　　1 teaspoon salt
2 cups cream　　　　　　　　　　Pepper to taste

Grease a 3–quart casserole dish. Peel and shred potatoes. Soak in ice-cold water to remove starch, then dry by placing on paper towels and patting out as much water as possible. Place potatoes in casserole dish and add salt and pepper. Cover with cream. Cover and bake at 325 degrees for 1½ hours. Uncover and continue to bake for 30 minutes, to brown potatoes. Serves 6 to 8.

PARSNIPS WITH BROWN BUTTER

1 pound parsnips　　　　　　　　2 tablespoons bread crumbs
2 to 3 tablespoons butter　　　　　1 tablespoon finely chopped fresh
Juice of ½ lemon　　　　　　　　　　parsley or chives
Salt and pepper to taste

Wash and peel parsnips. Cut into strips about ½ to ¾ inch in diameter, and in even lengths; set in steaming basket over boiling water. Cover and cook until tender but still firm. In a small frying pan, heat butter over low heat until brown (do not burn). Put butter in a large skillet; add parsnips and stir to coat. Cook for 3 to 4 minutes, stirring constantly, until the parsnips begin to brown. Add lemon juice, salt and pepper, bread crumbs, and parsley or chives. Toss and serve. Makes 6 servings.

HOLIDAY CARROTS

½ cup oil
1 cup brown sugar
1 cup flour
1 teaspoon baking soda
½ teaspoon baking powder
¼ teaspoon salt

2 cups grated carrots
Rind of 1 lemon, grated
3 tablespoons lemon juice
3 eggs
Cinnamon (optional)
Sugar (optional)

In a mixing bowl, beat together oil and brown sugar. Add flour, baking soda, baking powder, salt, carrots, lemon rind, lemon juice, and eggs. Mix well. Pour into a buttered 1-quart ring mold. Sprinkle with cinnamon and sugar, if desired. Bake at 350 degrees for 45 minutes or until set. Remove from oven and cool for a few minutes. When cool enough to handle, turn out onto a serving dish. Makes 4 to 6 servings.

BAKED STUFFED TOMATOES

2 firm, ripe tomatoes
¼ cup dry bread crumbs
2 teaspoons butter or margarine,
    melted
½ teaspoon grated Parmesan cheese

⅛ teaspoon basil, crumbled
⅛ teaspoon oregano, crumbled
1 teaspoon minced fresh parsley
Salt and pepper to taste

Cut tomatoes into halves. In a small bowl, mix thoroughly bread crumbs, melted butter or margarine, Parmesan cheese, basil, oregano, parsley, salt, and pepper. Press crumb mixture on top of each tomato half, and put in a greased 9-inch square baking dish. Bake at 350 degrees for 20 minutes. Topping should be light brown; if it is not, place tomatoes under broiler for a minute to two. Makes 4 servings.

SWEET PICKLED BEETS

2 or 3 bunches small, young beets
½ cup sugar
½ cup water
½ cup vinegar

¼ teaspoon cloves
¼ teaspoon allspice
¾ teaspoon cinnamon

Trim leaves from beets, leaving 3 inches of tops and roots on. Wash beets thoroughly. In a heavy pot, bring beets to a boil; reduce heat and simmer for 15 minutes or until skins slip off easily. Drain and put into cold water. Remove skins, tops, and roots. In a separate saucepan, combine sugar, water, vinegar, cloves, allspice, and cinnamon. Bring to a boil. Put cooked beets in a serving bowl and pour syrup on top. Mix well. Chill before serving. Makes 6 to 8 servings.

SPRING DANDELION GREENS

2 to 3 bunches fresh dandelion
  greens
½ pound sliced bacon

¼ cup bacon grease
⅓ to ½ cup vinegar

Use only fresh, tender dandelion leaves—no buds or flowers. Wash well and dry between paper towels. Set aside. Cut bacon slices in small pieces and fry until crisp. Drain on paper towels and crumble. Mix ¼ cup of the bacon grease with vinegar and heat to simmering point. Pour over greens. Sprinkle with bacon bits and toss.

Contributor's comment: "My great-great-grandmother Elizabeth Shupe was left at Winter Quarters, Nebraska, when her husband, Andrew Jackson Shupe, joined the Mormon Battalion and traveled with this U.S. Army troop to the West Coast. She and her children lived in a covered wagon, and she dug roots in the winter snow to help keep them alive. One of the dishes she prepared was dandelion greens wilted with hot grease and vinegar. Today many of her descendants (she eventually had sixteen children) still gather the first green leaves of the dandelion (they become bitter as soon as buds appear) and prepare this favorite pioneer salad."

ACADIA SLAW

1 medium head cabbage, shredded
¼ cup finely chopped green pepper
¼ cup finely chopped red pepper

⅔ cup mayonnaise
2 teaspoons prepared mustard
⅓ cup sugar

In a large bowl, toss together cabbage, green pepper, and red pepper. In a separate bowl combine mayonnaise, mustard, and sugar. Pour over cabbage mixture and toss. Chill before serving. Makes 10 servings.

Contributor's comment: "Acadian foods, a specialty in New Orleans, are a combination of the Creole and Cajun cultures. This recipe was handed down from my great-great-grandmother, Bettes."

AUNT IRIS'S ROLLS

2 package (1 tablespoon each) active
   dry yeast
½ cup warm water
1½ cups milk, scalded
⅔ cup shortening

½ cup sugar
1 tablespoon salt
2 eggs, beaten
1 cup mashed potatoes
4 to 5 cups flour

In a small bowl dissolve yeast in warm water; set aside. In a separate bowl mix together scalded milk, shortening, sugar, salt, eggs, and mashed potatoes. Stir in 1 cup flour and yeast. Gradually add remaining flour until dough is soft but not sticky. Cover with a clean dish towel, and let rise in a warm place until double in bulk. Punch dough down, then let rise again. Shape into rolls and place on greased cookie sheet. Cover and let rolls rise again. Bake at 350 degrees for 10 to 15 minutes, or until golden brown.

MORMON MUFFINS

2 cups water
5 teaspoons baking soda
1 cup shortening
2 cups sugar
4 eggs
1 teaspoon salt
5 cups flour

1 quart buttermilk
4 cups All Bran or Bran Buds
2 cups bran flakes
2 cups dates, raisins, or prunes,
    chopped
1 cup nuts, chopped (optional)

Bring water to boil and add baking soda; set aside to cool. In a large mixing bowl, cream shortening and sugar. Add eggs one at a time, blending thoroughly. Stir in salt. Add flour and buttermilk alternately. Mix in cooled water with baking soda. Stir well. In a separate bowl, combine bran cereals, fruit, and nuts. Fold into batter. Muffin batter is now ready to use or may be stored up to 30 days for later use. To store, pour batter into a container with a tight-fitting lid. Keep in refrigerator until ready to use.

To bake, spoon batter, without stirring, into greased muffin tins, or line muffin tins with paper baking cups. Fill muffin cups ¾ full. Bake at 375 degrees for 15 to 20 minutes. Makes 5 dozen muffins.

RHUBARB CRUNCH

1 cup granulated sugar
2 tablespoons cornstarch
1 cup water
1 teaspoon vanilla
1 cup rolled oats
½ cup flour

1 teaspoon cinnamon
¾ cup brown sugar
½ cup butter or margarine
4 cups (1½ pounds) diced rhubarb
Sweetened whipped cream

In a small saucepan, combine granulated sugar, cornstarch, and water. Cook, stirring, until thick and clear. Remove from heat and stir in vanilla; set aside. In a mixing bowl, combine rolled oats, flour, cinnamon, and brown sugar; cut in butter until crumbly. Put half the mixture onto bottom of greased 8–inch square baking pan. Cover with diced rhubarb. Pour sugar mixture over rhubarb. Top with remaining crumb mixture. Bake at 350 degrees for 45 minutes to 1 hour. Cut in squares and serve warm, plain or with sweetened whipped cream. Makes 8 servings.

PLYMOUTH PRUNE CAKE

1 cup prunes
1 cup water
1 cup butter (margarine or
    shortening may also be used)
2 cups sugar
3 eggs, beaten

3 cups flour
1 teaspoon baking soda
1 teaspoon cinnamon
1 teaspoon cloves
1 cup milk

Chop prunes and place in a small saucepan with 1 cup water. Bring to a boil; reduce heat and simmer for 20 minutes. Remove from heat. Strain, reserving ½ cup of juice, and set aside. In a large mixing bowl, cream butter, sugar, and eggs. Mix well. Stir or sift together flour, baking soda, cinnamon, and cloves. Add to creamed mixture alternately with milk. Add chopped prunes and ½ cup reserved prune juice. Pour into a greased and floured 9 x 13–inch baking pan. Bake at 350 degrees for 30 to 35 minutes.

CHOCOLATE POTATO CAKE

3 cups water
2 cups sugar
2 cups raisins
1 cup shortening
2 teaspoons cinnamon
½ teaspoon nutmeg
½ teaspoon cloves

3 cups flour
1 teaspoon salt
2 tablespoons cocoa
2 teaspoons baking soda
1 large potato, peeled and finely
   grated

In a large saucepan, combine water, sugar, raisins, shortening, cinnamon, nutmeg, and cloves. Bring to a boil, and boil for 5 minutes. Remove from heat and let cool. Stir or sift together flour, salt, cocoa, and baking soda. Add to cooled raisin mixture. Stir in grated potato and mix well. Place the mixture into a greased and floured 9 x 13-inch cake pan and bake 30 to 35 minutes at 350 degrees. Serve plain with a vanilla or lemon sauce, or frosted with chocolate frosting.

Contributor's comment: "Morgan is well known for its potato farms. When I was a child, potatoes were an every-night staple in our diet. My mother was creative in using them, as this cake indicates."

SOUR CREAM CAKE

1 cup sour cream
1 cup sugar
2 eggs, beaten
1¾ cups flour
¼ teaspoon salt
1 teaspoon baking soda

1½ teaspoons cocoa
1 teaspoon cinnamon
1 teaspoon nutmeg
1 cup raisins
1 cup nuts, chopped

In a large bowl, mix sour cream, sugar, and eggs. Stir or sift together flour, salt, baking soda, cocoa, cinnamon, and nutmeg; add to creamed mixture. Mix well. Stir in raisins and nuts. Pour batter into a greased and floured 9 x 13–inch baking pan. Bake at 350 degrees for 30 to 35 minutes.

Contributor's comment: "This recipe came from my mother, who would always make this cake for men who worked on our farm at harvest time."

BOILED RAISIN CAKE

2 cups water
2 cups raisins
2 teaspoons baking soda
1 cup shortening
2 cups sugar
2 eggs, beaten
1 teaspoon vanilla

3 cups flour
1 teaspoon baking powder
1 teaspoon salt
2 teaspoons cinnamon
1 teaspoon nutmeg
½ teaspoon cloves
Caramel Frosting (recipe below)

In a saucepan, bring water to boil; add raisins and baking soda and simmer for 10 minutes. Set aside. In a large mixing bowl, cream shortening, sugar, eggs, and vanilla. Stir or sift together flour, baking powder, salt, cinnamon, nutmeg, and cloves. Add hot raisin mixture to creamed mixture. Then add dry ingredients. Beat well (batter will be very thin). Pour into 2 greased and floured 9–inch round cake pans. Bake at 350 degrees for 30 to 35 minutes. Cool slightly before removing from pans. When completely cool, frost with Caramel Frosting.

CARAMEL FROSTING

1 cup brown sugar, firmly packed
½ cup butter or margarine
¼ cup milk

1½ teaspoons vanilla
2 cups confectioners' sugar

In saucepan over low heat, melt brown sugar and butter or margarine. Bring to a boil and cook, stirring continuously, for 2 minutes. Add milk and bring to boil again. Remove from heat, and cool thoroughly. Stir in vanilla and confectioners' sugar, and beat until frosting is smooth and of spreading consistency, adding additional confectioners' sugar if necessary.

APRICOT CAKE

4 cups canned or bottled apricots
2 teaspoons baking soda
½ cup hot water
1 cup sugar
1 cup oil
2 eggs
2 cups flour

½ teaspoon cloves
1 teaspoon cinnamon
1 teaspoon salt
1 teaspoon vanilla
1 cup nuts, chopped
Caramel Frosting (recipe on p. 127)

Drain apricots, reserving ½ cup juice. In blender or food processor, puree apricots with ½ cup juice; set aside. Dissolve baking soda in hot water; set aside. In a large mixing bowl, combine sugar, oil, and eggs. Blend well. Stir or sift together flour, cloves, cinnamon, and salt. Add to sugar/oil/egg mixture with dissolved baking soda and vanilla. Add nuts and pureed apricots. Mix well (batter will be thin). Pour into greased and floured 9 x 13–inch baking pan. Bake at 350 degrees for 30 to 35 minutes. Cool, then frost with Caramel Frosting.

Clockwise from top left: Edna's Chicken Noodle Soup (p. 118); Parmesan Bread Sticks (p. 12); Nana's String-Bean Stew (p. 142); Red and Green Chili (p. 99).

Top left: Black-Walnut Brownies (p. 44); Honey Nut Bars (p. 108). Top right: Divinity (p. 89); Peanut Butter Fudge (p. 89); Taffy-Pulled Butter Mints (p. 159); English Toffee (p. 47). Bottom, from left: Carrot Cookies (p. 180); Old-Time Cinnamon Jumbles (p. 197); Honey Peanut-Butter Cookies (p. 107); Molasses Sugar Cookies (p. 158).

OLD-FASHIONED BREAD PUDDING

¾ cup raisins
18 slices stale white bread, torn into
    bite-size pieces
3 cups milk
3 eggs, beaten
2 cups sugar
2 teaspoons vanilla

2 tablespoons flour
1 teaspoon baking powder
1 teaspoon ground cinnamon
½ teaspoon nutmeg
½ teaspoon salt
Ice cream
Caramel Sauce (recipe below)

Toss raisins and bread in large bowl. Place in greased 2½-quart casserole dish. Combine milk, eggs, sugar, and vanilla. Stir or sift together flour, baking powder, cinnamon, nutmeg, and salt. Add to milk mixture; mix well. Pour over bread and raisins. Bake at 325 degrees for 40 to 50 minutes. Serve pudding warm, topped with ice cream and Caramel Sauce. Makes 10 to 12 servings.

CARAMEL SAUCE

¼ cup cornstarch
¼ cup water
2 cups brown sugar

1¾ cups water
2 tablespoons butter or margarine
2½ teaspoons vanilla

Dissolve cornstarch in ¼ cup water; set aside. In a 3-quart saucepan, combine sugar, 1¾ cups water, butter, and vanilla. Stirring constantly over medium heat, bring to a boil. Gradually stir in cornstarch/water mixture. Heat, stirring constantly, until mixture comes to boil. Remove from heat and cool. Sauce may be served warm or cold. Makes about 3 cups.

POOR MAN'S PUDDING

⅔ cup uncooked rice
½ cup sugar
½ teaspoon cinnamon

2 quarts milk
⅔ cup seedless raisins
Nutmeg

In a saucepan, combine rice, sugar, cinnamon, milk, and raisins. Place over medium heat and, stirring constantly, heat until near boiling point. Remove from heat and pour into a well-buttered 3½- or 4-quart baking dish. Bake at 200 degrees for 2 to 3 hours. Stir 2 or 3 times during the first hour. Sprinkle the top with nutmeg, and continue cooking for additional 1 to 2 hours. Pudding is done when liquid is all absorbed.

Contributor's comment: "My grandmother Lettie Matilda Hammon Stoker was an industrious woman. Besides caring for her nine children, she helped her husband to market berries and other fruit from their farm in Roy. Often she would leave home early in the morning with the white-topped wagon loaded with fruit. A favorite food that could be prepared in her absence was Poor Man's Pudding. It was cooked slowly in the oven of the old kitchen range and became a family favorite."

RAISIN COOKIES

2 cups raisins
1 cup water
1 cup butter or margarine
1½ cups sugar
3 eggs
1 teaspoon vanilla

3½ cups flour
1 teaspoon salt
1 teaspoon baking soda
1 teaspoon cinnamon
1 cup nuts, chopped
Granulated sugar

In a small saucepan over medium heat, boil raisins and water until the water evaporates (check often so pan doesn't become dry, burning the raisins). Remove from heat and set aside. In a large mixing bowl, cream together butter or margarine and sugar. Add eggs and vanilla, and mix well. Stir in raisins. Stir or sift together flour, salt, baking soda, and cinnamon; add to creamed mixture. Stir in nuts and mix well. Form dough into balls the size of a walnut, roll in sugar, and place on greased cookie sheet. Bake at 375 degrees for 10 to 12 minutes. Makes 2 dozen cookies.

FESTIVAL PEACH PIE

1 baked 9–inch pie shell or 6 to 8
   baked tart shells
6 peaches, sliced
1 tablespoon lemon juice
½ cup sugar
Juice drained from fruit

Water
½ cup sugar
¼ cup cornstarch
1 tablespoon butter
¼ teaspoon salt
½ teaspoon almond extract

Prepare pie shell or tart shells, using favorite recipe. When baked, set aside to cool. Slice fresh peaches, and gently add lemon juice and ½ cup sugar. Let stand 1 hour.

Drain juice from peaches; measure and add water, if necessary, to make 1 cup. Pour into a medium-size saucepan. In a small bowl, mix ½ cup sugar and cornstarch. Stir into juice, and bring to a boil over medium heat. Stirring constantly, cook until thickened. Add butter, salt, and almond extract. Fold in peaches, and pour into baked pie shell or tart shells. Serve with sweetened whipped cream, if desired.

FRESH PEACH ICE CREAM

3 cups mashed fresh peaches
2 tablespoons lemon juice
2 cups whipping cream

3 cups sugar
Juice from 1 orange
3½ cups milk

Combine all ingredients, mixing well. Freeze in 4–quart ice cream freezer, following manufacturer's directions.

7 · GREAT SALT LAKE COUNTRY

Great Salt Lake Country is home to the capital of Utah, Salt Lake City. With nearly a million people in Salt Lake County, the area is the most densely populated in the state as well as the cultural center. Salt Lake City offers almost everything a major metropolis can: the Utah Symphony, Utah Opera Company, Ballet West, several acting companies, and many museums and galleries. It is also home to several educational institutions, including the University of Utah, known internationally for the Jarvik 7, the first artificial heart.

The University of Utah was established in 1850, demonstrating the commitment of the Mormon pioneers to education and cultural advancement. This was just three years following Utah's first permanent settlement in 1847. Resourceful and committed to self-sufficiency, the settlers established basic industries to supply all their needs. By 1862, U.S. troops had established a military base at Fort Douglas, east of the city, to protect communications and transportation routes. For many decades, Salt Lake City was the last major supply point for westbound travelers.

Great Salt Lake Country extends west to the Nevada border, encompassing vast tracts of mostly uninhabitable land, including the Great Salt Lake Desert. Tooele County, almost seven thousand square miles in size, has fewer than thirty thousand residents. Historically, the economy of the area west of Salt Lake Valley has depended on mining and smelting. In 1864, soldiers from Fort Douglas started mining in the Oquirrh Mountains, and more than five hundred claims were staked in that year alone. Silver, lead, zinc, and gold worth millions of dollar were taken, but the most famous mineral discovered was copper. Today the Kennecott (Bingham) Copper Mine is the world's largest excavation—almost two miles across and deeper than two Empire State Buildings sitting one on top of the other.

The area continues to be a regional mining hub, but now there are many other major industries in or near Salt Lake City, from pharmaceuticals to candy production. Salt Lake County leads the state in trade, transportation, communications, finance, insurance, and construction.

There are many interesting places to visit in Salt Lake City. In the heart of the city is Temple Square, the state's most popular tourist attraction. On the ten-acre square are visitor centers, the Salt Lake Mormon Temple, and the Tabernacle, home of the 350–voice Mormon Tabernacle Choir. Nearby are the Beehive House and the Lion House, homes of Utah colonizer Brigham Young; several buildings housing the Mormon Church's headquarters; the church's Genealogical Library, the largest repository of its kind in the world; and the Museum of Church History and Art. Other major tourist attractions include the Utah State Capitol; Pioneer Trail State Park with a recreated mid-1800s community; Hogle Zoo; Hansen Planetarium; and two major sports centers: the Delta Center, where the Utah Jazz of the National Basketball Association play, and Franklin Quest Field, a minor-league baseball park.

While this area is the most cosmopolitan in the state, it is not without natural beauty. West of the capital city is the Great Salt Lake, the second saltiest body of water in the world and the largest lake in the United States west of the Mississippi. To the east, the city extends into the foothills of the Wasatch Mountains, which offer hiking, fishing, camping, and skiing. The tram at one of the area's many ski resorts, Snowbird, offers an exceptional way to view Utah's rugged mountains in summer or winter, rising nearly 3,000 feet from the base to the top.

Great Salt Lake Country has a rich culinary history. Many foods served today in homes and restaurants came from recipes brought to Utah by Mormon pioneers and converts from the eastern United States and Europe. The earliest pioneers became resourceful in supplementing their meager crops with plants and nuts indigenous to the area, such as berries, pine nuts, watercress, and sego roots.

Later arrivals introduced ethnic specialties, and today the metropolis boasts restaurants serving Italian, Chinese, Greek, French, Mexican, Indian, and other international cuisines. But the pioneer traditions are also being preserved, and many favorite dishes reflect this heritage. Whether it's Barley and Pine Nut Casserole or Fresh Corn Pie, Mom's Stuffed Green Peppers or Watercress Salad, Orange Rhubarb or Grandpa Pete's Pumpkin Pie, you'll find delicious dishes to add to your own cooking repertoire from the good cooks of Great Salt Lake Country!

SUNDAY ROASTED CHICKEN

1 roaster-fryer (3 to 4 pounds)
1 rib celery, cut in half
1 onion, quartered

3 tablespoons butter
Salt and pepper
Paprika

Remove giblets and neck from inside cavity of chicken. Rinse chicken inside and out; drain and pat dry. Put celery and onion inside cavity. Rub butter on outside of chicken and season with salt, pepper, and paprika. Place on two pieces of heavy-duty foil that are crossing each other. Wrap foil tightly around chicken, being careful not to tear foil, and fold the ends well. Place in a large roasting pan, and bake at 450 degrees for 1 hour. Turn off heat, but leave chicken in oven for an additional 2 hours or more. When ready to serve, open foil and brown chicken under broiler. Serve hot or cold.

Contributor's comment: "Chicken prepared this way can be especially useful if you have to be away from home for a while. As long as you have just one hour of time available before you leave, chicken can be cooked and then left in the oven until you return and are ready to eat."

STUFFED PORK CHOPS

4 pork chops, cut 1–inch thick
1 cup bread crumbs
½ teaspoon salt
¼ teaspoon pepper
2 teaspoons minced fresh parsley

¼ teaspoon sage
2 teaspoons grated onion
¼ cup finely diced apples
6 tablespoons milk

Cut a pocket vertically in each chop. In a mixing bowl combine bread crumbs, salt, pepper, parsley, sage, onion, apples, and milk. Mix well. Stuff each chop with bread mixture. Place in shallow baking pan and bake at 350 degrees for 1 hour or until tender. Makes 4 servings.

PAULA'S BARBECUE SAUCE

2 cups catsup	⅓ cup Worcestershire sauce
1½ cups water	¼ cup butter or margarine
Juice of 2 lemons	Salt to taste
2 tablespoons sugar	Tabasco sauce to taste

Combine all ingredients and bring to a boil. Simmer 4 to 6 hours. Use immediately or store in refrigerator in airtight container. Makes about 4 cups sauce.

To prepare barbecued chicken or pork chops: Marinate boneless pork ribs or chicken breasts in barbecue sauce for 1 hour before cooking. Cook on barbecue grill, basting frequently, or wrap tightly in aluminum foil and bake at 350 degrees for 1 hour. Remove foil and brown meat under broiler.

Contributor's comment: "I find this is an excellent recipe to use for a large crowd. The barbecued meat is delicious served steaming hot, and still great when the kids come back for a snack later."

TYLER'S LANDMARK CHILI

1 pound coarsely ground beef	¼ teaspoon black pepper
1 onion, chopped	1½ teaspoons salt
¾ cup water	1 teaspoon cumin
¼ teaspoon red pepper	1 or 2 chili pods, ground (optional)
½ teaspoon garlic powder	⅓ cup catsup
1 teaspoon chili powder	1 can (24 ounces) chili beans
1 teaspoon paprika	

In a skillet over medium-high heat, brown meat and onions. Add water, red pepper, garlic powder, chili powder, paprika, black pepper, salt, cumin, ground chili pods, and catsup. Simmer, uncovered, for 15 minutes. Add chili beans and bring to a boil. Remove from heat and serve. Makes 4 servings.

Contributor's comment: "This chili was served at Tyler's Ice Cream, a restaurant in Murray from 1935 to 1954. The recipe came from a former Greek resident of Bingham Canyon, a mining community on the western side of Salt Lake Valley, who had operated a cafe in San Juan Teotihuacan, Mexico."

GREAT SALT LAKE JERKY

¾ teaspoon salt
¼ teaspoon cracked pepper
1 tablespoon brown sugar
1 garlic clove, crushed

2 tablespoons soy sauce
1 tablespoon Worcestershire sauce
1 pound lean meat, thinly sliced (see
    note below)

In a small bowl, combine all ingredients except meat. Mix well. Arrange meat slices in a single layer on a clean flat surface. Spread both sides generously with salt mixture. Place the meat strips in a tightly covered glass, stoneware, plastic, or stainless steel container; cover tightly. Place in refrigerator for 6 to 12 hours, stirring occasionally. Drain. Place meat in single layer on a baking sheet, and place in oven set at 150 degrees for 6 to 12 hours. Meat should be hard and crisp with no evidence of moisture. When meat is thoroughly cooled, store it in a glass container with a tight lid.

Note: Game meats, such as deer, elk, and antelope, can be used in making jerky. Any cut can be used, but the loin, round, and flank cuts are preferred. As a precaution against disease, freeze game meats for at least 60 days at 0 degrees centigrade before drying.

FRONTIER JERKY

1 teaspoon salt
¼ teaspoon pepper
1 teaspoon garlic powder
2 tablespoons Worcestershire sauce

2 tablespoons liquid smoke
1 pound lean meat, thinly sliced (see
    note above)

Follow directions for preparing Great Salt Lake Jerky.

Contributor's comment: "We don't grow much around Tooele and the Great Salt Lake desert but salt. Jerky and saltwater taffy are favorite recipes in our area."

BARLEY AND PINE NUT CASSEROLE

2 tablespoons butter
⅓ cup pine nuts*
¼ cup butter
1 cup barley
1 onion, chopped
½ cup minced fresh parsley

¼ cup minced green onions
¼ teaspoon salt
¼ teaspoon pepper
2 cans (14 ounces each) beef or
   chicken broth

Over medium heat, melt 2 tablespoons butter; add pine nuts and stir until lightly toasted. Remove nuts to a small dish and set aside. In the pan in which nuts have been toasted, melt ¼ cup butter. Add barley and onion and, stirring constantly, sauté until tender. Remove pan from heat and stir in toasted pine nuts, parsley, green onions, salt, and pepper. Spoon into 1½–quart casserole. (Casserole may be prepared ahead to this point and refrigerated.) In a small saucepan, bring the broth to boiling. Stir into barley mixture. Bake at 375 degrees for 1 hour. Makes 4 servings.

*Note: Slivered almonds may be used if pine nuts are not available.

FRESH CORN PIE

Pastry for 2-crust 9–inch pie
6 cups fresh corn
¼ cup plus 2 tablespoons half-and-
   half

1 tablespoon sugar
Salt and pepper to taste
¼ cup butter or margarine

Prepare pastry for two-crust pie, using your favorite recipe. Line a 9–inch pie plate with bottom crust; roll out top crust; set aside. In a large bowl, combine corn, half-and-half, sugar, salt, and pepper. Pour into pastry-lined tin. Dot with butter. Adjust top crust over filling, making several slits so steam can escape. Bake at 400 degrees for 15 minutes; reduce heat to 375 degrees and bake for an additional 45 minutes. Makes 6 to 8 servings.

GREEN BEANS AND SOUR CREAM

1 pound green beans
1 tablespoon butter or margarine
½ pound fresh mushrooms, sliced,
 or 1 can (8 ounces) sliced mushrooms

1 cup sour cream
Salt and pepper to taste
Paprika to taste

Cook green beans in salted water until tender. Drain well and set aside. In a heavy skillet, melt butter and sauté mushrooms over medium heat. Add sour cream, salt, pepper, and paprika. Simmer for 2 to 3 minutes; do not boil, as sauce will curdle. Add beans and mix well. Makes 6 servings.

NANA'S STRING-BEAN STEW

2 pounds boneless beef or lamb stew
 meat
2 tablespoons olive oil
⅓ cup flour
Salt and pepper to taste
3 cloves garlic, crushed
2 cups water
1 can (28 ounces) diced tomatoes

4 medium carrots, peeled and cut
 into 2-inch pieces
4 medium potatoes, peeled and
 quartered
1 large onion, cut in eighths
2 pounds fresh green beans*
1½ cups water
1 teaspoon baking soda

In a large roasting pan, heat oil. Dredge meat in flour, salt, and pepper, turning to coat evenly. Brown in hot oil. When meat is browned, stir in garlic, then 2 cups water and tomatoes. Mix well. Cover pan, and bake at 350 degrees for 1½ hours or until meat is tender. Stir in carrots, potatoes, and onions. Return to oven and bake 30 minutes or until vegetables are tender. In a large pot, combine 1½ cups water and baking soda. Add green beans and bring to a boil. Simmer, covered, until tender, about 20 to 25 minutes. Drain and stir into oven-baked stew. Makes 6 to 8 servings.

*Note: Canned green beans may be used instead of fresh green beans. Drain well 2 16-ounce cans beans and stir into stew.

BAKED RICE AND CHEESE

6 eggs, separated
2 cups cooked rice
1 cup milk

1 cup grated cheddar cheese
¼ cup butter or margarine, melted
Salt and pepper to taste

In a mixing bowl, beat egg yolks. Stir in rice, then milk, cheese, and melted butter or margarine. In a separate bowl, beat egg whites to soft peaks. Fold egg whites into rice mixture. Add salt and pepper. Pour into a greased 2–quart casserole dish. Bake uncovered at 375 degrees for 30 to 35 minutes, or until top is crusty brown. Makes 8 servings.

CABBAGE ROLLS

1½ pounds lean ground beef
½ cup rice, partially cooked
¼ cup chopped onion
1 egg

1 teaspoon salt
¼ teaspoon pepper
12 to 16 outer cabbage leaves
1 can (28 ounces) tomatoes

Mix together meat, rice, onion, egg, salt, and pepper. Form into sausage-shape rolls. Wash cabbage leaves and steam until slightly wilted. Place meat mixture in center of each cabbage leaf and roll. Fold leaf loosely, allowing room for meat and rice to swell. In a large skillet, place a few remaining raw cabbage leaves. Over these leaves, arrange layers of stuffed cabbage rolls with seam down. Cover with tomatoes. Cover pan and simmer for 1 hour, or bake at 350 degrees for 1½ hours. Makes 10 to 12 servings.

MOM'S STUFFED GREEN PEPPERS

6 medium-size green bell peppers
1½ pounds lean ground beef
1 cup soft bread crumbs
1 egg
½ cup water

1 tablespoon Worcestershire sauce
1 small onion, diced
2 cloves garlic, crushed
Salt and pepper to taste
1 can (8 ounces) tomato sauce

Cut off tops of peppers and remove seeds. Rinse and set aside. In a large mixing bowl, combine ground beef, bread crumbs, egg, water, and Worcestershire sauce. Stir in onion, garlic, salt, and pepper; mix well. Spoon into green peppers. Rub oil over the outside of green peppers, and place in a roasting pan. Bake, covered, at 350 degrees for 50 minutes. Remove lid and pour tomato sauce over each pepper. Bake for another 10 minutes. Makes 6 servings.

SUNDAY FAMILY OMELET

5 or 6 medium potatoes
½ cup vegetable oil
1 large onion, chopped
1 green pepper, chopped
2 cups chopped ham

Salt and pepper to taste
12 eggs, beaten
½ cup water
¾ cup grated cheddar cheese

Wash and peel potatoes; dice into small cubes. In a large skillet, fry potatoes in oil over medium heat for 7 to 10 minutes. Add onion and green pepper. Sauté until vegetables are tender. Stir in ham and salt and pepper. In a mixing bowl, beat eggs and water. Pour over potato mixture and stir gently until egg is evenly distributed. Reduce heat to simmer and cover skillet for 2 to 3 minutes, or until egg starts to set. Uncover and gently turn omelet with spatula. Cook additional 2 to 3 minutes, until omelet is cooked evenly on top and bottom. Remove from heat. Sprinkle cheese on top, and cover with lid for 2 minutes to melt cheese. To serve, cut into pie-shaped wedges. Makes 6 to 8 servings.

SCALLOPED POTATOES

6 medium potatoes, peeled and
   sliced
1 medium onion, sliced
2 tablespoons flour

2 cups whole or evaporated milk
Salt and pepper to taste
3 tablespoons butter or margarine

In a 2–quart greased casserole dish, layer potatoes and onion. In a jar, combine flour, milk, salt, and pepper. Screw lid on tightly and shake well until smooth. Pour milk mixture over potatoes, and dot with butter. Bake uncovered at 350 degrees for 1 hour. Makes 6 servings.

HOTEL UTAH BORSCHT

4 cups beets with juice, pureed
2 cups chicken stock
1 teaspoon salt
1 teaspoon Áccent
2 teaspoons fresh lemon juice

2 tablespoons cornstarch
½ cup water
2 cups sour cream
4 egg yolks
2 hard-cooked eggs, finely chopped

In a large pot, combine pureed beets, chicken stock, salt, Áccent, and lemon juice; bring to a boil. Dissolve cornstarch in cold water and add to hot liquid. Boil slowly for 5 minutes. In a separate bowl, combine sour cream and egg yolks. Stir in 1 cup of the hot beet broth, then stir sour-cream mixture into broth. Bring to a boil, then remove immediately from heat. Chill. To serve, sprinkle finely chopped hard-cooked eggs over cold soup. Makes 6 to 8 servings.

Comment from co-author Joanne Milner: "My grandfather Antonio Furano worked for over forty years as a chef and head saucier at the Hotel Utah in downtown Salt Lake City. He had an innate gift in culinary art. He cooked according to taste, as he had been taught by his mother in Italy. He knew exactly which seasonings and spices to use for enhanced flavor, and used the palm of his hand to measure ingredients. His specialties were served to world, national, and local dignitaries. Chef Gerard, head chef of the Hotel Utah, once said, 'Tony is the best chef on sauces and soups in the United States.' Hotel Utah Borscht and the two recipes that follow—Tony's Spaghetti and Meatballs, and Hotel Utah Green Salad Dressing—are the only written recipes I have from him."

TONY'S SPAGHETTI AND MEATBALLS

SPAGHETTI SAUCE:
2 cans (28 ounces each) tomatoes
2 cans (6 ounces each) tomato paste
1½ cups water
1 teaspoon salt
½ teaspoon oregano
2 tablespoons finely chopped fresh
    basil, or 2 teaspoons dried basil
    leaves
MEATBALLS:
2 pounds ground beef
½ pound ground veal

½ pound ground pork
1 teaspoon salt
½ teaspoon pepper
3 eggs
2 tablespoons grated Parmesan
    cheese
2 cups soft bread crumbs
2 tablespoons finely chopped fresh
    parsley
1 large clove garlic, crushed
½ cup water
1 tablespoon olive oil

Prepare spaghetti sauce: In a heavy saucepan, bring tomatoes to a boil. In a separate saucepan, dilute tomato paste with water and stir over medium heat until smooth. Add tomato paste mixture to tomatoes. Stir in salt, oregano, and basil. Bring to a boil. Reduce heat and cover pot. Simmer, stirring occasionally, until sauce is thick. This will take at least 1 hour.

While sauce is cooking, prepare meatballs: In a large bowl, combine ground beef, veal, and pork. Add salt, pepper, eggs, Parmesan cheese, bread crumbs, parsley, and garlic. Mix together, adding water to moisten. Form into balls. Heat a large, heavy skillet, and add olive oil. Fry meatballs until golden brown, being careful not to cook too fast.

Pour sauce over meatballs and simmer uncovered for about 20 minutes. Serve over hot cooked spaghetti. Makes 6 to 8 servings.

HOTEL UTAH GREEN SALAD DRESSING

1 large clove garlic, minced
1 tablespoon salt
1 tablespoon sugar
1 teaspoon pepper

3 cups tomato juice
4 cups olive oil
2 cups red wine vinegar

Combine all ingredients and beat for 15 minutes. Refrigerate. Makes 9 cups dressing. Before using, shake dressing well, then pour over tossed salad greens.

WATERCRESS SALAD

4 bunches watercress
8 slices bacon
1 cup olive oil
⅓ cup cider vinegar
1 tablespoon sugar
1 teaspoon paprika
1 teaspoon salt

1 teaspoon Worcestershire sauce
½ teaspoon horseradish
½ teaspoon pepper
¼ teaspoon prepared mustard
1 ice cube
8 green onions, chopped

Wash watercress and pat dry. Put in a plastic bag and refrigerate 1 hour. Meanwhile, cook bacon until crisp. Drain well on paper towels; crumble and set aside. In a mixing bowl, combine olive oil, vinegar, sugar, paprika, salt, Worcestershire sauce, horse-radish, pepper, and mustard. Add ice cube and beat until well blended. In a large salad bowl, toss watercress, bacon, and onions. Add dressing and serve immediately. Makes 8 servings.

Contributor's comment: "For an authentic pioneer Sunday night supper, start with a salad of wild greens gathered along the ditch bank. Serve a main dish of boiled sucker fish or jackrabbit accompanied by sego roots. End the meal with service berries or other wild berries."

CARROT AND RAISIN SALAD

2 cups carrots, finely grated
½ cup raisins
⅓ cup sour cream

1 tablespoon honey
¼ cup walnuts, chopped

In a bowl combine carrots and raisins. In a separate bowl, mix sour cream and honey. Stir into carrots and raisins. Add nuts. Mix well. Makes 4 to 6 servings.

ORANGE RHUBARB

1½ pounds rhubarb
1 cup sugar

1½ cups water
1 medium-large orange

Wash, drain, and trim rhubarb; cut into 1–inch pieces. In a large saucepan, combine rhubarb, sugar, and water. Peel orange and scrap away as much white underpeel as possible. Break into segments, and cut each segment into fourths. Add to rhubarb. Bring to a boil, then simmer, covered, for 10 minutes. Serve warm or cold. Makes 4 to 6 servings.

RHUBARB WITH STRAWBERRIES

3 pounds rhubarb
3 cups water
2 cups sugar

2 cups fresh strawberries or 1 package (10 ounces) frozen whole strawberries

Wash, drain, and trim rhubarb; cut into 1–inch pieces. In a large, heavy saucepan, combine rhubarb, water, and sugar. Cook over medium heat, stirring frequently, about 20 minutes. Remove from heat. Stir in fresh or frozen berries. If fresh or unsweetened frozen berries are used, add additional sugar if desired. Stir until well mixed. Refrigerate until ready to serve. Makes 8 to 10 servings.

VERNICE'S WHEAT ROLLS

2 packages (2 tablespoons) active
   dry yeast
½ cup sugar
½ cup warm water
½ cup butter (no substitute)

½ cup boiling water
1 cup cold water
3 eggs, beaten
5 cups whole wheat flour
1½ teaspoons salt

Dissolve yeast and sugar in ½ cup warm water. Place butter in a large mixing bowl, and add boiling water to melt it. Stir in 1 cup cold water. Add beaten eggs, then yeast mixture. Sift flour and salt together, and stir into liquid mixture. Beat well. Cover bowl with damp cloth and let dough rise in a warm place until double in bulk. Stir down. Knead slightly on a floured board; then divide into 3 portions for convenient handling. Shape into rolls and place close together on buttered baking pan. Cover loosely with a clean dish towel and let rise until double in bulk. Bake at 400 to 425 degrees for 12 to 15 minutes, until golden brown. Makes 2½ to 3 dozen rolls.

Contributor's comment: "This recipe is from my loving friend Vernice Rosenvall, who was co-author of the cookbook Wheat for Man: Why and How. *She established a reputation as one who knew how to use stone-ground wheat in baking and cooking. She demonstrated her techniques widely in an effort to help people use stored wheat in everyday food preparation."*

FRENCH BREAD

2 packages (2 tablespoons) active dry yeast	2 tablespoons sugar
1 cup lukewarm water	3 teaspoons salt
2 cups hot water	8 cups flour
2 tablespoons shortening	Evaporated milk
	Sesame seeds (optional)

Dissolve yeast in 1 cup lukewarm water; set aside. In a large mixing bowl, combine hot water, shortening, sugar, and salt. Stir to dissolve sugar and melt shortening; cool to lukewarm. Add yeast to shortening mixture. Blend in 4 cups flour and beat until well blended. Add remaining flour to make moderately stiff dough. Knead until satiny and well mixed. Cover and let rise in a warm place until double in bulk, punching down occasionally.

On a floured board, divide dough into four balls; let rest 10 minutes. Roll out each part of dough into a rectangle about 9 inches x 12 inches. Roll the dough up, starting from the long side; pinch the ends to seal. Place on a greased cookie sheet. Cover lightly with a clean dish towel, and let rise 1½ hours, or until almost double in size.

Score top of loaf with a sharp knife. Brush with evaporated milk and sprinkle with sesame seeds, if desired. Bake at 400 degrees until golden brown, about 30 minutes. Makes 4 loaves.

ELIZA'S BANANA-NUT BREAD

½ cup butter or margarine
1 cup sugar
2 eggs
2 cups mashed ripe banana

2 cups flour
1 teaspoon baking soda
¼ teaspoon salt
1 cup walnuts, chopped

Cream together butter, sugar, and eggs. Stir in mashed bananas. Stir or sift together flour, baking soda, and salt. Add to banana mixture, and mix thoroughly. Stir in nuts. Pour into greased and floured 9 x 3 x 5–inch loaf pan or three small loaf pans. Bake at 350 degrees for 35 to 45 minutes. Turn out on rack and cool before slicing.

Contributor's comment: "This recipe is from my dear neighbor Eliza Faucett, a real pioneer, who baked this bread for her family and friends each week until her eyesight dimmed at the age of ninety-seven."

SHERAN'S CHOCOLATE APPLESAUCE CAKE

½ cup butter or margarine
1 cup sugar
1 egg
1 teaspoon vanilla
1 cup applesauce
½ cup water
1½ cups flour

⅓ cup cocoa
1½ teaspoons baking soda
1 teaspoon salt
1 teaspoon cinnamon
¼ teaspoon cloves
¼ teaspoon nutmeg

Cream butter or margarine, sugar, and eggs. Add vanilla, applesauce, and water. Stir or sift together flour, cocoa, baking soda, salt, cinnamon, cloves, and nutmeg. Add to applesauce mixture, and mix well. Pour into a greased and floured 9 x 5 x 3–inch loaf pan. Bake at 350 degrees for 45 minutes. Turn out on wire rack and cool.

ANNA'S APPLE STREUSEL

1 package (1 tablespoon) active dry
    yeast
½ teaspoon sugar
¼ cup warm water
½ cup milk
¼ cup oil
¼ cup sugar

½ teaspoon salt
1 egg
1¾ to 2 cups flour
3 or 4 large apples, peeled and sliced
¼ cup sugar
½ teaspoon cinnamon
Streusel Topping (recipe below)

In a bowl, combine yeast, sugar, and warm water; stir to dissolve. Set aside. In a saucepan, scald milk. Add oil, sugar, and salt; stir to dissolve sugar. Pour milk mixture into a large mixing bowl, and add egg and 1 cup of the flour to make a paste. Stir in yeast mixture. Add remaining flour to make a soft dough. On a floured board, roll out dough about ½ inch thick. Place dough on a greased cookie sheet, and let rise in a warm place for 10 minutes.

Place apple slices in a mixing bowl. Combine cinnamon and sugar, and sprinkle over apples. Mix well. Arrange apple mixture on dough and sprinkle with Streusel Topping (recipe below). Bake at 350 degrees for 20 minutes. Serve warm or cold with sweetened whipped cream or vanilla ice cream. Makes 12 servings.

STREUSEL TOPPING

½ cup flour
½ cup sugar

½ teaspoon cinnamon
¼ cup butter or margarine

In a bowl, combine flour, sugar, and cinnamon. Cut butter or margarine into flour mixture to resemble size of peas. Sprinkle on Apple Streusel as directed above.

OATMEAL CAKE

3 cups boiling water
2 cups rolled oats
1 cup shortening
2 cups granulated sugar
2 cups brown sugar
4 eggs, beaten

3 cups flour
2 teaspoons baking soda
1 teaspoon salt
1 teaspoon cinnamon
Coconut Topping (recipe below)

Combine water and oats and let stand 20 minutes. In a separate bowl, cream shortening, granulated sugar, brown sugar, and beaten eggs. Stir in oat mixture. Stir or sift together flour, baking soda, salt, and cinnamon; add to oat mixture. Mix well. Pour into a greased and floured 9 x 13–inch baking pan. Bake at 350 degrees for 35 to 40 minutes. Remove from oven. While cake is still warm, spread on Coconut Topping.

COCONUT TOPPING

½ cup butter or margarine
1 cup brown sugar
½ cup evaporated milk

1 teaspoon vanilla
1 cup coconut
¾ cup nuts, chopped

In a heavy saucepan, combine butter or margarine, brown sugar, and evaporated milk. Bring to a boil over medium heat; boil for 1 minute. Remove from heat, and stir in vanilla, coconut, and nuts. Spread on warm Oatmeal Cake.

DAD'S DUTCH APPLE PIE

Pastry for single-crust 9–inch pie
4 cups tart apple slices
¾ cup sugar
½ teaspoon cinnamon
¼ teaspoon nutmeg

¾ cup flour
½ cup brown sugar, firmly packed
½ teaspoon cinnamon
½ cup butter or margarine
Sweetened whipped cream

Using your favorite recipe, prepare pastry for single-crust 9–inch pie; set aside. Wash, peel, and slice apples. Combine with sugar, ½ teaspoon cinnamon, and nutmeg. Mix well. In a separate bowl, blend flour, brown sugar, cinnamon, and butter or margarine to make coarse crumbs. Spoon apples into pastry-lined pie tin. Place crumb mixture on top of apples. Bake at 425 degrees until apples are done, about 45 minutes. Serve warm or cold with sweetened whipped cream.

GRANDPA PETE'S DEEP-DISH PUMPKIN PIE

2 unbaked pie shells (recipe below)
2 cups pumpkin, canned or cooked
½ cup honey
½ cup brown sugar
3 eggs
½ teaspoon salt
1 teaspoon cinnamon

½ teaspoon ginger
¼ teaspoon nutmeg
⅛ teaspoon cloves
1 cup evaporated milk
1 cup whole milk
Sweetened whipped cream

Prepare pie shells (recipe below); refrigerate until ready to fill. In a large mixing bowl, combine pumpkin, honey, and brown sugar. Add eggs one at a time, and mix well. Stir in salt, cinnamon, ginger, nutmeg, and cloves. Add evaporated and whole milk. Mix until smooth. Pour into prepared pie shells. Bake at 450 degrees for 10 minutes; then reduce heat to 350 degrees and bake for an additional 50 minutes, or until knife inserted in center comes out clean. Cool. Serve with sweetened whipped cream. Makes 2 pies.

WANNY'S FLAKY PASTRY

2 cups flour
1 cup butter or margarine

1 egg
3 tablespoons fresh lemon juice

Sift flour into mixing bowl. Cut butter or margarine into flour until mixture resembles small peas. Beat egg with lemon juice and add to flour-margarine mixture, tossing lightly with fork. Mix only until blended. Divide dough into 3 balls, and refrigerate for 30 minutes. Roll each ball out into a circle to fit a 9–inch pie plate. Carefully place in pie plate and flute edges. Prick bottom and sides with a fork. Refrigerate until ready to use. Then bake at 425 degrees for 12 to 15 minutes, or until golden. Makes 3 pie shells.

For Grandpa Pete's Pumpkin Pie: Line 2 pie plates with pastry and flute edges. Refrigerate until ready to fill. Proceed as directed above. Third pie shell may be refrigerated or frozen for future use.

Contributor's comment: "Pete Montoya was a wonderful neighbor and friend. A master gardener, he could be found from early morning until late evening tilling the ground, planting seeds, and pulling weeds for his neighbors. His generous service was rendered at no charge, but he did enjoy an occasional home-baked pie from my kitchen. Pumpkin was his favorite."

BUTTERSCOTCH PIE

1 baked 9-inch pastry shell	¾ cup brown sugar
¾ cup granulated sugar	2 egg yolks, beaten
2 tablespoons cornstarch	¼ teaspoon salt
3 tablespoons flour	1 teaspoon vanilla
2 cups milk	Meringue or sweetened whipped
3 tablespoons butter	cream

Prepare pastry shell using your favorite recipe; bake, then set aside to cool. In a saucepan, combine granulated sugar, cornstarch, flour, and milk. Stir over medium heat until thickened and smooth. Set aside. In a skillet melt butter and brown sugar until bubbly and caramelized, taking care not to let it burn. Pour into thickened sugar/milk mixture. Add beaten egg yolks and stir over low heat until mixture starts to bubble. Cook, stirring constantly, for 1 minute longer. Remove from heat and add salt and vanilla. Pour into baked pastry shell. If using meringue, prepare before chilling pie. If using sweetened whipped cream, chill pie first and add whipped cream just before serving.

To make meringue: Beat 2 egg whites with ¼ teaspoon cream of tartar until foamy and double in volume. Add 2 to 3 tablespoons sugar, one tablespoon at a time, beating all the while at high speed until sugar is dissolved and meringue stands in firm peaks. Spread meringue on pie filling, being sure to seal it to the shell, and swirl into design of peaks and valleys. Place under preheated broiler for 3 to 5 minutes, until peaks brown to a delicate golden color. Chill pie before serving.

LILIAN'S BAKEWELL TARTS

Bakewell Tart Pastry (recipe below)
½ cup shortening
1½ cups sugar
2 eggs
1 cup milk

1 teaspoon vanilla
2½ cups flour
1 teaspoon salt
3 teaspoons baking powder
Favorite jam

Prepare pastry for tarts (recipe below). Set aside. In a mixing bowl, cream shortening, sugar, and eggs. Add milk and vanilla. Stir or sift together flour, salt, and baking powder. Add to creamed mixture, and mix well. Put a teaspoon of jam on pastry round in each muffin cup, and fill cups ⅔ full with cake batter. Bake at 375 degrees for 20 to 25 minutes. Cool, then frost with confectioners' sugar frosting and decorate with candied cherries, nuts, or coconut. Remove carefully from tins to serve.

BAKEWELL TART PASTRY

1½ cups flour
¼ teaspoon salt

½ cup shortening
4 tablespoons ice water

Combine flour and salt in a mixing bowl. Cut shortening into flour. Add ice water, and mix well. Roll out pastry as for pie crust. Grease 24 medium-size muffin-tin cups. Measure diameter of bottom of cup and add ½ inch. Using an inverted glass equal to that size, cut pastry into rounds to cover bottom of muffin cup and extend up sides ¼ inch. Proceed as directed above. Makes 24 tarts.

MOLASSES SUGAR COOKIES

¾ cup shortening
1 cup sugar
¼ cup molasses
1 egg, beaten
2 cups flour

½ teaspoon salt
2 teaspoons baking soda
1 teaspoon cinnamon
½ teaspoon cloves
¼ teaspoon ginger

In a saucepan melt shortening over low heat. Cool. Add sugar, molasses, and egg. Beat well. Stir or sift together flour, salt, baking soda, cinnamon, cloves, and ginger. Add to creamed mixture and mix well. Chill dough for 30 minutes. Form into 1–inch balls, roll in sugar, and place on ungreased cookie sheet. Bake at 375 degrees for 8 to 10 minutes. Makes 4 dozen.

SALTWATER TAFFY

1 cup sugar
2 tablespoons cornstarch
¾ cup light corn syrup
½ cup water

½ teaspoon salt
2 tablespoons butter
2 teaspoons vanilla

Grease a 9 x 9 x 2–inch baking pan. In a 1½–quart saucepan, mix sugar and cornstarch. Stir in corn syrup, water, and salt. Add butter. Cook over medium heat, stirring constantly, until mixture boils and sugar is completely dissolved. Continue cooking, without stirring, until temperature reaches 260 degrees on a candy thermometer, or until a small amount of mixture dropped into very cold water forms a ball that is hard enough to hold its shape, yet pliant. Remove from heat, and stir in vanilla. Pour into prepared pan. Let stand until cool enough to handle. Butter fingers and pull taffy until it has satin-like finish and light color. Pull into long strips, ½–inch wide. With scissors, cut into 1–inch pieces. Wrap individual candies in wax paper. Makes 1 pound.

TAFFY-PULLED BUTTER MINTS

2 cups sugar
1 cup water
¼ cup butter
⅛ teaspoon cream of tartar

Few drops of food color (optional)
4 to 5 drops oil of peppermint or
  wintergreen

Combine sugar, water, butter, and cream of tartar in a heavy saucepan. Stir over medium heat until sugar is dissolved. Heat mixture to hard-ball stage (260 degrees on a candy thermometer) without stirring. If sugar crystals form on sides of pan, wipe them off with a damp pastry brush. Pour candy onto buttered marble slab or buttered large shallow pan. With buttered hands, turn edges of candy into center so they won't get hard. Let cool. When cool enough to handle, sprinkle with a few drops of food color and choice of flavoring. Pull and fold several times to incorporate color and flavoring. Continue pulling and folding until candy is almost cold. Stretch out in a rope of even thickness, about ½- to ¾-inch wide. Cut in short, bite-size lengths. Makes 1 pound.

8 · MOUNTAINLAND

Mountainland is appropriately named, for national forest land accounts for two-thirds of the region, while lakes, fields, and picturesque mountain communities make up the rest. Utah Lake is the West's largest natural freshwater lake, while Mirror Lake, an alpine lake high in the Uinta Mountains, attracts tens of thousands of summer outdoor enthusiasts. The 22,000 acres of Wasatch Mountain State Park, Utah's largest state park, provides year-round recreational activities and breathtaking scenery. Over a million visitors visit Mountainland each year to enjoy the region's natural beauty and tranquillity.

This area was the northernmost point reached by early Spanish explorers, the Dominguez-Escalante expedition, in 1776. In the eastern part of the continent, the American colonists were fighting for independence, while in the west, explorers were sending reports to the King of Spain describing the "most pleasing, beautiful, and fertile spot in all of New Spain."

At the time of this expedition, the region was inhabited by the peaceful Utes who lived around Utah Lake. They were gradually expelled when fur trappers entered the area in the 1820s and the Mormon settlers arrived beginning in the late 1840s. Soon communities surrounded by farms and ranches dotted the valleys.

In the mid and late nineteenth century, the major industry in the region's Wasatch Mountains was mining, with rich lodes of silver, lead, and zinc. Park City, founded in 1872, grew rapidly when a high-grade silver ore was discovered. During the next half-century, silver worth more than $400 million dollars was extracted from the mines. By the 1950s the mines had played out, but Park City soon found an equally valuable resource: snow. Today skiers from around the world can be found on the slopes of the ski resorts in the area, while others enjoy cross-country skiing and snowmobiling at Wasatch Mountain State Park.

The region is definitely a fun one to visit, with a wide variety of attractions for every season. Numerous canyons are within easy reach of freeways and country roads, with hiking and backpacking trails; fishing and boating on lakes and reservoirs; a wide variety of wildflowers and wildlife; waterfalls and springs. Among the many scenic drives popular from spring to fall are the Alpine Loop, a 24–mile drive that winds around the east slope of Mt. Timpanogos, and the 38–mile Nebo Loop, which climbs to elevations over 9,000 feet between Payson and Nephi. A 1.5–mile hike in American Fork Canyon leads to Timpanogos Cave, a national monument with over forty types of cave formations. Children of all ages enjoy riding on the "Heber Creeper," a steam-powered train that runs between lower Provo Canyon and the Heber Valley, skirting around Deer Creek Reservoir.

Cultural attractions abound in Mountainland. Many art galleries line the streets of Park City, which is also home to the Kimball Art Center and host of a summer arts festival that attracts more than 100,000 people. Park City is also the site of the internationally acclaimed Sundance Film Festival. The western side of the region, in and around Provo, attracts visitors and residents to the Springville Museum of Art and Brigham Young University's Museum of Art; America's largest Fourth of July celebration, the Freedom Festival; an annual international folk dance festival and a storytelling festival; and community fairs and other celebrations.

Utah County, whose county seat is Provo, has recently become a center for major software and other computer-related industries, boosting the economy and the population significantly. Brigham Young University, with an enrollment of more than twenty-five thousand students, is also in Provo.

Recipes from Mountainland reflect the diverse nature of the area. The Heber Valley, sometimes called "Little Switzerland" because of the mountainous setting and the many Swiss immigrants who settled there, sponsors Swiss Days each year. Crowds flock to Midway to view parades, programs, and art exhibits, and sample Swiss culinary specialties.

Good cooks in the region rely upon the bounteous crops and herds of livestock to supply their dinner tables. Among their favorite recipes are such hearty main courses as Barbecued Beef Short Ribs, Sweet and Sour Lamb, Fluffy Chicken Casserole, and Mexicali Meat Loaf. Potatoes, which grow well in the rocky soil of the mountains, are spotlighted in Golden Potato Bake and Beulah's Potato Salad. Those with a sweet tooth will enjoy Shelby's Dutch Apple Pie, Fresh Cherry Cobbler, and Apricot Ice Cream. All feature products grown in Mountainland, home of some of the most beautiful mountains and valleys in the world.

BARBECUED BEEF SHORT RIBS

3 pounds beef short ribs
1 onion, chopped
2 tablespoons fat or oil
2 tablespoons sugar
½ cup water
1 teaspoon prepared mustard

1 teaspoon salt
¼ cup vinegar
1 cup catsup
3 tablespoons Worcestershire sauce
½ cup celery slices

In a large, heavy skillet, brown short ribs with onion in hot fat or oil. Combine remaining ingredients and add to ribs. Cover pan, and cook slowly for 1½ to 2 hours, or until tender. Makes 4 to 6 servings.

SPARERIBS AND SAUERKRAUT

6 to 7 pounds pork loin country-
style spareribs
Salt and pepper
3 cans (16 ounces each) mild
sauerkraut
1½ cups coarsely chopped apples

1 medium onion, coarsely chopped
8 whole cloves
2 to 4 tablespoons brown sugar
¼ teaspoon pepper
1½ cups chicken broth
Chopped fresh parsley

Preheat broiler. Arrange ribs in a shallow roasting pan; sprinkle all sides with salt and pepper to taste. Broil 6 inches from heat, browning all sides (about 30 minutes). Reduce oven temperature to 325 degrees. Drain sauerkraut thoroughly. In a deep, heavy roasting pan, combine sauerkraut with apples, onion, cloves, brown sugar, ¼ teaspoon pepper, and chicken broth. Arrange ribs on top, pushing them into the sauerkraut. Cover and bake for 2 hours, basting ribs often with juices. If needed, add more chicken broth. To serve, transfer ribs and sauerkraut to a large platter; sprinkle with parsley. Makes 6 to 8 servings.

CHERRY-GLAZED CHICKEN

1 broiler-fryer chicken, cut up, or 6
   chicken breast halves, skinned
   and boned
½ cup milk
½ cup all-purpose flour
1 teaspoon dried thyme
Salt and pepper to taste

1 to 2 tablespoons vegetable oil
1 can (16 ounces) unsweetened pie
   cherries
¼ cup brown sugar
¼ cup granulated sugar
1 teaspoon prepared mustard

Rinse chicken; pat dry with paper towel. Pour milk into a shallow bowl. In another container, combine flour, thyme, salt, and pepper. Dip chicken first in milk, then in flour mixture; coat evenly. Heat oil in large skillet. Add chicken; brown on all sides. Put chicken in a 13 x 9–inch baking dish; cover with aluminum foil. Bake at 350 degrees for 30 minutes.

While chicken is baking, drain cherries, reserving ½ cup juice. In a saucepan, combine cherries, reserved juice, brown sugar, and granulated sugar; mix well. Bring mixture to a boil over medium heat. Add mustard; mix well. Simmer for 5 minutes or until slightly thickened.

After chicken has baked 30 minutes, remove baking dish from oven. Remove cover, and spoon hot cherry mixture evenly over chicken. Return uncovered dish to oven and bake at 350 degrees for 15 minutes, or until chicken is done. Serve immediately. Makes 6 servings.

FLUFFY CHICKEN CASSEROLE

1 chicken (3 to 4 pounds)
SAUCE:
½ cup butter
¾ cup flour
4 cups chicken broth
2 cups milk
4 eggs, beaten
DRESSING:
3 tablespoons butter or margarine
1 cup diced celery

1 cup diced onion
16 slices bread, crumbled
1 teaspoon baking powder
1 teaspoon salt
½ teaspoon pepper
1 teaspoon dried sage
½ teaspoon poultry seasoning
4 eggs
Fine bread crumbs

Prepare chicken: Remove giblets from chicken; rinse well. Place chicken in a large pot, and cover with water and salt to taste. Bring to boil, then simmer until tender. Strain, reserving broth, and remove chicken skin and bones. Cut chicken into pieces. Set aside.

Prepare sauce: In a large skillet, melt butter or margarine and add flour. Stir over medium heat until smooth and bubbly. Add warm chicken broth, milk, and eggs. Stir until mixture is thick and fluffy. Set aside.

Prepare dressing: In a large skillet, heat butter or margarine. Add celery and onion, and sauté. Set aside. In a large bowl, combine bread, baking powder, salt, pepper, sage, and poultry seasoning. Add celery and onions; blend well. Beat eggs and fold into dressing.

Spoon dressing into a 4–quart greased casserole dish. Cover with a small amount of sauce. Spread chicken pieces over sauce and cover with remaining sauce. Sprinkle with bread crumbs. Cover and bake at 350 degrees for 50 minutes. Makes 6 to 8 servings.

MEXICALI MEAT LOAF

1¼ pounds ground beef
¾ cup rolled oats
½ cup tomato juice
1 egg
1 teaspoon salt

½ teaspoon pepper
½ cup chopped onion
1 teaspoon chili powder
Mexicali Sauce (recipe below)
Green or red pepper rings

In a bowl, combine ground beef, rolled oats, tomato juice, egg, salt, pepper, onion, and chili powder. Pack into a shallow 2–quart oblong baking dish. Bake uncovered at 350 degrees for 30 minutes.

While meat loaf is baking, prepare Mexicali Sauce (recipe below). Remove meat loaf from oven and drain off excess juices. Pour topping over partially cooked meat loaf, and place green or red pepper rings on top. Bake an additional 30 minutes. Cool 10 minutes before cutting. Makes 6 to 8 servings.

MEXICALI SAUCE

3 tablespoons butter
3 tablespoons flour
1 teaspoon salt
1½ cups milk

½ pound medium sharp cheese,
   cubed
1 can (12 ounces) Mexicorn

Melt butter in saucepan. Add flour and salt; stir until smooth. Blend in milk. Bring to boil, and cook 1 minute. Add cheese; stir until melted, then add corn.

SWEET AND SOUR LAMB

3½ pounds lamb, cubed (leftover
    roast lamb may be used)
1 tablespoon oil
1 can (16 ounces) pineapple chunks
    and juice
3 tablespoons cornstarch

3 tablespoons vinegar
6 tablespoons water
1 tablespoon soy sauce
½ cup brown sugar
1 green pepper, cut in bite-size pieces
Hot steamed rice

In a large skillet, brown lamb in oil, then drain off fat. Strain pineapple, and add juice to meat. Combine cornstarch, vinegar, water, soy sauce, and brown sugar; mix well. Add to meat mixture and stir. Add pineapple chunks and green pepper. Heat and serve over hot rice.

Contributor's comment: "The livestock industry is very important in our area, with many families depending upon raising lamb and beef as a livelihood. I selected this particular recipe because it is a different and delicious way to serve lamb. About thirty years ago the Summit County Wool Growers Auxiliary started having a lamb supper in October to promote the use of lamb. At the supper, lamb is prepared and served in a variety of ways, such as roast leg of lamb, barbecued lamb chops, and lamb meat loaf with sage dressing. Sweet and Sour Lamb is a favorite dish."

BEEF CRUST PIE

1 pound lean ground beef
½ cup chopped onion
½ cup chopped green pepper
½ cup soft bread crumbs
½ cup tomato sauce
1½ teaspoons salt

⅛ teaspoon pepper
⅛ teaspoon oregano
2 cups cooked rice
½ cup tomato sauce
½ teaspoon salt
1 cup grated cheese

In a bowl, combine beef, onion, green pepper, bread crumbs, ½ cup tomato sauce, 1½ teaspoons salt, pepper, and oregano. Mix well. Pat into a 9–inch pie plate, covering bottom and sides to form crust.

Combine cooked rice, ½ cup tomato sauce, ½ teaspoon salt, and ¼ cup of the cheese. Mix well. Spoon mixture into beef crust. Cover with aluminum foil and bake at 350 degrees for 30 minutes. Remove from oven. Remove foil, and sprinkle remaining cheese over top of pie. Return to oven and bake, uncovered, an additional 5 minutes, or until cheese is melted. Makes 6 servings.

GOLDEN POTATO BAKE

6 medium potatoes
2¼ cups grated sharp cheddar
    cheese
1 bunch green onions, chopped
1 teaspoon salt

⅛ teaspoon pepper
2 cups sour cream
¼ cup milk
2 tablespoons butter, melted
⅓ cup fine bread crumbs

Wash potatoes well. Boil in salted water until tender. Drain and cool. Peel and grate potatoes into a large bowl. Add cheese, onions, salt, pepper, and sour cream mixed with milk. Mixture should be quite moist, so 1 or 2 tablespoons additional milk may be added, if needed. Mix well. Spread in a greased 9 x 13–inch pan or baking dish. In a small saucepan, melt butter over medium heat; stir in bread crumbs and mix until coated with butter. Sprinkle on top of potatoes. Bake uncovered at 300 degrees for 50 minutes. Makes 8 servings.

LIMA BEAN AND HAM SOUP

1 cup dried lima beans	1 large onion, chopped
6 cups water	1 teaspoon dry mustard
1 ham bone	Salt and pepper to taste
2 ribs celery, sliced	Chopped parsley

Combine lima beans and water in a kettle and bring to a boil. Boil for 2 minutes. Remove from heat, cover, and let stand 1 hour. Add ham bone, celery, and onion; cover and simmer until beans are tender, about 1½ hours. Check occasionally while beans are cooking, and add more water, if needed. Season with dry mustard, salt, pepper, and parsley. Remove ham bone and cut off any meat; add to soup and reheat. Makes 6 to 8 servings.

GRANDMA GALLIS'S DEER NOODLE SOUP

2 cups flour	2 cups deer meat, cooked and cubed
2 eggs	1 onion, chopped
¼ teaspoon salt	4 cups tomato juice
¼ cup milk	Salt and pepper to taste

Prepare noodles: Place flour in a mixing bowl, and make a well in center. Add eggs, salt, and milk. Stir with fork. Knead with hands until dough is stiff. Divide into 3 portions. On a floured board, roll each portion of dough very thin; dust with flour. Carefully roll dough up and cut into thin strips. Separate noodles and spread to dry.

Prepare soup: In a large kettle, simmer deer meat and onion in tomato juice for 30 minutes. Add salt and pepper. Add noodles and cook, covered, for 20 minutes. Makes 4 to 6 servings.

BEULAH'S POTATO SALAD

5 large potatoes
7 hard-cooked eggs
6 or 7 green onions, chopped
2 cups Miracle Whip

½ recipe Beulah's Salad Dressing
   (recipe below)
Milk
Paprika

Wash potatoes and cook in boiling water until tender. Drain and cool. Remove skins and cut potatoes into cubes in a large mixing bowl. Peel eggs; set 2 eggs aside and chop the other 5. Add chopped eggs and green onions to potatoes. Combine Miracle Whip with ½ recipe of Beulah's Salad Dressing, thinning mixture with 2 or 3 tablespoons milk. Mix until well blended. Pour over potatoes and eggs, and mix thoroughly. Slice 2 reserved eggs; arrange slices on top of salad, and sprinkle with paprika. Cover and refrigerate a few hours so flavors blend. Makes 6 to 8 servings.

BEULAH'S SALAD DRESSING

⅔ cup vinegar
⅓ cup water
1 teaspoon flour
½ cup sugar
1½ teaspoons salt

¼ teaspoon pepper
1 teaspoon dry mustard
2 eggs, slightly beaten
1 tablespoon butter

In a saucepan, bring vinegar and water to boil. Combine flour, sugar, salt, pepper, and dry mustard, and stir into boiling vinegar, stirring constantly. Pour small amount of hot mixture into beaten eggs; blend thoroughly. Stir into remaining mixture in saucepan, and cook additional 2 or 3 minutes. Add butter and remove from heat. Cool thoroughly. Use half of dressing in potato salad. Put remaining dressing in a tightly covered jar and refrigerate for future use. Makes 1½ cups.

FAMOUS CLAM CHOWDER

1 pound sliced bacon
4 cans (6½ ounces each) clams,
   minced or chopped
¾ cup chopped onion
4 cups peeled and diced potatoes
2 cups water

1 cup chopped celery
½ cup shredded carrot
4 cups half-and-half
3 tablespoons flour
1 tablespoon parsley flakes
Salt and pepper to taste

Strain clams, reserving juice. Set aside. With scissors or sharp knife, cut bacon into small pieces. Place in a large, heavy pan. Fry over medium-high heat until almost crisp. Drain off bacon fat, and add onion, potatoes, clam juice, and water. Bring to a boil and add celery and carrots. Boil for 5 to 7 minutes, or until vegetables are tender but firm. Add 3 cups of the half-and-half. Stir. In a bowl, mix flour with remaining cup of half-and-half. Stir into chowder. Add salt, pepper, clams, and parsley. Bring to a boil over low heat, stirring frequently. Remove when boiling point is reached so clams don't overcook. Makes 6 to 8 servings.

MOLASSES BRAN BREAD

2 cups whole bran cereal
2 cups buttermilk
1 cup raisins
½ cup boiling water
½ cup molasses

¼ cup brown sugar
2 tablespoons oil
2 cups flour
2 teaspoons baking soda
¼ teaspoon salt

In a bowl, soak bran in buttermilk. In a separate bowl, cover raisins with boiling water and let stand 10 minutes. Drain. In a large bowl combine molasses, brown sugar, oil, and raisins. Stir in flour, baking soda, and salt. Add bran mixture, and mix well. Pour into 2 greased and floured 7 x 4 x 2–inch loaf pans. Bake at 350 degrees for 50 to 55 minutes.

HENEFER'S HEAVENLY ROLLS

1½ packages (1½ tablespoons) active
   dry yeast
¼ cup lukewarm water
1 teaspoon salt
2 tablespoons sugar

3 cups sifted flour
1 cup butter or margarine
2 eggs
⅓ cup half-and-half
1 teaspoon vanilla

Combine yeast and lukewarm water; let stand until yeast is dissolved, about 5 minutes. Add salt and sugar. Place flour and margarine or butter in a large bowl. Rub the flour and butter mixture together until it is crumbly. In another bowl, beat eggs. Stir in half-and-half and vanilla, then yeast mixture. Stir well. Add flour-butter mixture. Stir well to form a dough just stiff enough to handle.

Turn dough onto a floured board and knead well until smooth and satiny. Roll the dough to ¼ inch in thickness and cut into desired shapes for rolls. Place rolls on a greased baking sheet. Cover with a clean dish towel and let rise in a warm place for about 30 minutes. Bake at 400 degrees for 10 to 12 minutes, or until tops are golden brown. Makes 2 dozen rolls.

HOOTENANNY PANCAKES

½ cup margarine or butter
9 eggs
1½ cups milk

½ teaspoon salt
1½ cups flour

Cut butter or margarine into pieces and place in a 9 x 13-inch baking dish. Place dish and butter in hot oven (375 degrees). While butter or margarine is melting, combine in a separate bowl the eggs, milk, salt, and flour. Beat until smooth. Pour mixture immediately into hot baking pan with the melted butter. Bake at 375 degrees for 20 minutes. Serve with fresh fruit, hot syrup, or jam. Makes 6 to 8 servings.

DATE-NUT BREAD

1 cup dates, chopped
1½ cups water
1 cup sugar
1 tablespoon butter or margarine
1 egg, beaten

1 teaspoon baking soda
1 teaspoon salt
2 cups plus 2 tablespoons flour
1 teaspoon vanilla
½ cup nuts, chopped

In a saucepan, combine dates, water, sugar, and butter or margarine. Boil for 5 minutes. Cool. Add beaten egg. Stir or sift together baking soda, salt, and flour. Stir into date mixture. Add vanilla and nuts. Mix well. Pour into a greased and floured 7 x 4 x 2–inch loaf pan. Bake at 350 degrees for 50 to 60 minutes, or until cake tester, inserted in center, comes out clean. Cool in pan 10 minutes; remove to wire rack to finish cooling. Wrap in foil.

ZUCCHINI BREAD

2 cups sugar
3 eggs
1 cup oil
2 teaspoons vanilla
2 cups grated zucchini
3 cups flour

½ teaspoon baking powder
1 teaspoon baking soda
1 teaspoon salt
1 cup raisins
1 cup nuts, chopped

In a large bowl, cream sugar, eggs, oil, and vanilla. Add zucchini and mix well. Stir or sift together flour, baking powder, baking soda, and salt. Add to zucchini mixture, and stir to blend. Add raisins and nuts. Pour batter into 2 floured and greased 7 x 4 x 2–inch loaf pans. Bake at 350 degrees for 50 or 60 minutes, or until cake tester, inserted in center, comes out clean. Cool in pan 10 minutes; remove to wire rack to finish cooling. Wrap in foil.

BERTHA'S RAISIN CREAM PIE

Pastry for 2 double-crust 9–inch pies
4 cups raisins
2 cups water
3 eggs, beaten

3 cups heavy cream
2 cups milk
2 tablespoons cornstarch
3 tablespoons lemon juice

Prepare pastry for 2 double-crust pies, using favorite recipe. Line pie plates, and roll out tops. Set aside. In a saucepan, combine raisins and water. Boil for 10 minutes. Drain and cool. In a bowl, combine eggs and cream. Stir in raisins. In a jar or other container with a tight lid, combine milk with cornstarch and shake until smooth. Pour into raisin-cream mixture. Add lemon juice and mix well. Pour into 2 pastry-lined pie plates. Cover with top pastry, and make several slits for steam to escape. Bake at 425 degrees for 30 to 35 minutes or until crust is lightly browned.

Contributor's comment: "This was a favorite pie of my dad, who always said that anything tastes good with enough sugar and cream, even woodchips."

WILVA'S FLAKY PASTRY

2 cups flour
¼ teaspoon baking powder
½ teaspoon salt

1 cup shortening
½ cup cold milk

In a bowl, combine flour, baking powder, and salt. Cut shortening into dry ingredients until mixture resembles small peas. Add cold milk and mix with fork until moistened and mixture follows fork around bowl. Roll out on floured board. Makes enough pastry for 2 9-inch pastry shells or 1 double-crust pie.

Contributor's comment: "The dough will be less sticky if you let it set a few minutes before rolling it out."

ANGEL MERINGUE PIES

4 egg whites, room temperature
½ teaspoon cream of tartar
½ teaspoon vanilla
1 cup sugar
4 egg yolks
½ cup sugar
3 tablespoons lemon juice

1 tablespoon grated lemon rind
  (optional)
¼ teaspoon salt
2 cups heavy cream (divided)
½ cup nuts, ground
Maraschino cherries

Cover a baking sheet with heavy, ungreased paper, such as kraft or parchment paper. Outline on paper 9 circles, each 4 inches in diameter, leaving a little space between circles. Set aside. Beat egg whites until foamy. Add cream of tartar and vanilla, and continue beating until soft peaks form when beater is removed from meringue. Add 1 cup sugar gradually, about 1 tablespoon at a time, and continue to beat until very stiff peaks form. Spread meringue over circles on paper and hollow out center, making a nest in each circle. Use spoon to shape shells or pipe through a pastry tube. Bake at 275 degrees for 45 minutes. Leaving oven door closed, turn off heat and let meringue shells dry about 1 hour. Remove from oven and gently peel off paper. Set meringues aside.

Beat egg yolks slightly. Stir in ½ cup sugar, lemon juice, lemon rind, and salt. Cook in top of double boiler over boiling water until thick enough to mound when dropped from spoon, about 8 to 10 minutes. Remove from heat and cool. Whip 1 cup of the cream; fold in cooled lemon filling. Fill meringue shells. Chill in refrigerator about 24 hours. Just before serving, whip remaining 1 cup cream, adding sugar to taste. Garnish meringue pies with sweetened whipped cream, ground nuts, and a maraschino cherry. Makes 9 servings.

SHELBY'S DUTCH-OVEN APPLE PIE

2¼ cups sugar
1 teaspoon cinnamon
½ cup cornstarch
⅛ teaspoon nutmeg
½ teaspoon salt

5 cups water
5 teaspoons lemon juice
3 pounds tart apples, pared, cored,
   and sliced
Pastry (recipe below)

Prepare pie filling: In large saucepan, blend sugar, cinnamon, cornstarch, nutmeg, and salt. Stir in water. Stirring constantly, cook until thick and bubbly. Remove from heat and add lemon juice. Pie filling may be used immediately or bottled and processed for later use. To bottle, pack apples into 3 hot, sterilized quart jars. Fill with hot syrup to neck of bottle. Wipe tops of bottles with clean cloth; screw lids on tightly. Process in boiling water bath 20 minutes. Make 3 quarts pie filling; 1 quart fills a 9-inch pie.

To prepare pie: Prepare pastry (recipe below). On a floured board, roll out one-half of the dough and line a 9–inch pie plate. Fill pastry shell with 1 quart pie filling. Roll out remaining dough. Puncture top crust with your own pie symbol, or make several slits for steam to escape. Place over top of filling, and seal edges.

To bake pie: Place three jar rings in bottom of Dutch oven. Set pie on top of rings. Cover oven with lid, and bake pie over a hot fire, using 8 coals, for 20 minutes. Leave 6 coals under bottom of oven and, using tongs, carefully place remaining coals on lid of Dutch oven. Continue baking for additional 40 to 50 minutes, until crust is golden brown.

DUTCH-OVEN PIE PASTRY

2⅔ cups flour
1 cup shortening

1 teaspoon salt
7 to 8 tablespoons cold water

Measure flour and salt into bowl. Cut in shortening until mixture resembles small peas. Sprinkle in water 1 tablespoon at a time. Mix lightly with a fork after each addition until all flour is moistened and dough begins to stick together. Makes enough pastry for 2 double-crust pies or 4 pie shells.

FRESH CHERRY COBBLER

4 cups fresh sour cherries, washed
   and pitted*
1 cup sugar
1 tablespoon instant tapioca
1 teaspoon vanilla
1 tablespoon lemon juice

1 cup flour
1 cup sugar
½ cup milk
1¼ teaspoons baking powder
½ cup butter or margarine

In a saucepan, combine cherries, 1 cup sugar, tapioca, vanilla, and lemon juice. Stirring frequently, heat over medium-low heat until sugar is dissolved. Mix together flour, 1 cup sugar, milk, and baking powder. Melt butter in 9-inch square baking dish in 350-degree oven. Pour batter on top of melted butter, and spoon cherries on top of batter. Bake uncovered at 350 degrees for 30 to 35 minutes.

*Note: 4 cups canned or bottled sour cherries may be used instead of fresh cherries. Drain and proceed as directed.

CHERRY CASHEW COOKIES

1 cup butter or margarine, softened
¾ cup granulated sugar
¾ cup brown sugar
2 eggs
1 teaspoon vanilla

2¼ cups flour
1 teaspoon baking soda
1 cup white-chocolate baking chips
1½ cups dried tart cherries
1 cup lightly salted cashews, chopped

In a large mixing bowl, combine butter, granulated sugar, brown sugar, eggs, and vanilla. Beat with mixer at medium speed until thoroughly mixed. Combine flour and baking soda; gradually add to creamed mixture. Stir in baking chips, cherries, and cashews. Drop by rounded tablespoonfuls onto ungreased baking sheet. Bake at 375 degrees for 12 to 15 minutes, or until golden brown. Let cool on wire racks. Store in a tightly covered container. Makes 4 dozen.

GRANDMA'S DATE-NUT FILLED COOKIES

2 cups chopped dates or raisins
⅔ cup sugar
⅔ cup water
½ cup chopped walnuts
1 cup shortening
2 cups brown sugar

2 eggs
½ cup buttermilk
1 teaspoon vanilla
3½ cups sifted flour
½ teaspoon salt
1 teaspoon baking soda

Prepare filling: In a saucepan, combine dates, sugar, water, and walnuts. Bring to a boil over medium heat, and cook, stirring constantly, until thick. Remove from heat and set aside.

Prepare cookie dough: Cream together shortening and brown sugar. Add eggs, buttermilk, and vanilla; mix well. Stir or sift together flour, salt, and baking soda. Add to creamed mixture, and mix well.

Assemble cookies: Drop dough by teaspoonfuls onto ungreased baking sheet. With thumb, make a small indentation in each cookie; fill indentation with ½ teaspoon filling. Place ½ teaspoon cookie dough on top of filling; press dough together with fingers to cover and seal the filling. Bake at 400 degrees until light brown, about 15 minutes. Makes 3 to 4 dozen cookies.

CARROT COOKIES

1 cup cooked and mashed carrots	2 cups flour
¾ cup butter or margarine	½ teaspoon salt
¾ cup sugar	2 teaspoons baking powder
2 eggs	Orange Butter Icing (below)

Cook and mash carrots; set aside. In a mixing bowl, cream butter or margarine, sugar, and eggs. Add carrots and blend. Stir or sift together flour, salt, and baking powder. Add to carrot mixture; mix well. Drop by teaspoonfuls on ungreased cookie sheet. Bake at 375 degrees for about 10 minutes. Remove cookies from cookie sheet and cool on wire racks. Then frost with Orange Butter Icing. Makes 2 dozen cookies.

ORANGE BUTTER ICING

2½ tablespoons butter	4 teaspoons orange juice
1½ cups confectioners' sugar	2 teaspoons grated orange rind

Cream together butter or margarine and confectioners' sugar. Stir in orange juice and orange rind. Mix well.

APRICOT ICE CREAM

4 cups pureed apricots	3 cups sugar
Juice of 2 oranges	1 teaspoon vanilla
Juice of 2 lemons	Pinch of salt
2 cans (12 ounces each) evaporated milk	2 cups heavy cream

Mix together pureed apricots, orange juice, and lemon juice. Stir in evaporated milk, sugar, vanilla, and salt. Whip cream and add to apricot mixture. Freeze in 4–quart freezer, following manufacturer's directions.

9 · PANORAMALAND

In the center of Utah lies Panoramaland, named for the colorful sandstone formations found there. The Native Americans called the area the "land of the sleeping rainbow," for the beautiful hues of yellow, purple, red, and white found in the rock. The land has a rich ancient past; where lava once flowed, rock formations alive with sagebrush and cedar remain. Fossil beds have replaced the ancient sea, and where there was once an enormous sandbar, an incredible 60,000–acre ever-moving sand dune exists today.

Capitol Reef National Park, which has been termed "America's most undiscovered park," combines the fairyland formations of Bryce Canyon National Park with the majestic stone masses of Zion National Park in an incredible area that has more color than either and is larger than both combined.

Evidence of inhabitants in the area dates back more than seven thousand years, to a Folsom Early Man site found in the Sevier Desert. The Fremont Indian culture disappeared around A.D. 1300, leaving mounds north of Nephi that today are considered among the most important Fremont agricultural sites extant. The Fremont Indians State Park houses a collection of artifacts from this fascinating culture, which existed in the area for nearly two thousand years.

In more recent times, the Utes, Paiutes, Goshutes, San Pitch, and other tribes inhabited the area, and in 1776, the Dominguez-Escalante expedition passed through. But, as with many other locations in Utah, the first permanent settlement occurred in the 1850s under guidance of the Mormon Church. In fact, due to its central location, Brigham Young selected Fillmore as the territorial capital. The legislature met there several times before voting in 1856 to move to the capital to Salt Lake City. One other group also inhabited the region for a time. During World War II, the federal government established a relocation center for Japanese-Americans at Topaz. Close to nine thousand internees lived at the center, making it the region's largest "city" for several years.

The economy of this area has long been based primarily on farming and ranching. At the turn of the century, Nephi was such a thriving livestock distribution center that some called it "Little Chicago." Hay and grains are grown on many farms, while alfalfa has proved uniquely successful, providing 90 percent of the state's alfalfa crop. And Sanpete County ranks among the country's top ten turkey-producing counties and the top twenty sheep-producing counties.

In 1869 precious metals—gold, silver, copper, lead, and zinc—were discovered around Tintic, and by end of the nineteenth century the area's mines had produced metals worth over $35 million. By the 1950s most of the mines had closed, though a few remain today.

Panoramaland offers a wide variety of scenic attractions, including four national forests, one national park, and four state parks. Fishermen are drawn to Fish Lake, famous for mackinaw, splake, and rainbow trout; and a herd of buffalo roam the Henry Mountains. In Marysvale Canyon is the Big Rock Candy Mountain, the only formation of its kind in the world and popularized in a folk song by Burl Ives. And for those interested in rural architecture, Spring City is the only town in Utah where every building is on the National Historic Register.

The region celebrates its history in several ways. In July Manti attracts thousands of visitors to Utah's biggest outdoor pageant, *The Mormon Miracle*, presented against the backdrop of the Mormon Church's Manti Temple. Harvest Homecoming Days in Capitol Reef National Park celebrates the bountiful orchards in Fruita, a turn-of-the-century community whose apple, pear, cherry, apricot, and peach trees are still maintained by an orchard management program. Other special observances include Sanpete County's Scandinavian Festival, Moroni's Turkey Days, and Fountain Green's Lamb Days.

The recipes from Panoramaland feature many of the foods served at these festivals and in the area's homes: turkey, lamb, and venison; potatoes, carrots, cabbage, and corn; and apples served in several ways.

MORONI'S FAMOUS BARBECUED TURKEY

Turkey tenders, breasts, or cut-up
   pieces
1 cup soy sauce
1 cup salad oil

2 cups 7–Up, Sprite, or other carbonated lemon-lime beverage
1½ tablespoons garlic powder
1½ to 2 tablespoons horseradish

In a bowl, combine soy sauce, salad oil, carbonated beverage, garlic powder, and horse-radish. Mix well. In a large dish, cover turkey with sauce. Cover and marinate overnight in refrigerator. Remove meat from sauce, reserving sauce. Cook on grill over medium coals, brushing occasionally with sauce.

Contributor's comment: "Sanpete County is the largest turkey-producing county in Utah. Turkey dishes are served at the 'Mormon Miracle Pageant' in July, almost every family reunion, lots of church suppers, and almost any other kind of gathering. Sanpete is also the state's largest sheep-producing county, so lamb dishes are popular."

APPLE CURRY MARINATED LAMB

1 5–pound lamb roast, rolled and fat
   trimmed
1 cup applesauce
2 teaspoons curry powder

¼ teaspoon freshly ground black
   pepper
2 teaspoons fresh lemon juice
1 teaspoon salt

Combine applesauce, curry powder, pepper, lemon juice, and salt. Mix well. Place lamb in a large container; spoon marinade over meat. Cover container and place in refrigerator. Marinate lamb roast in refrigerator 8 hours or longer, but no longer than 24 hours. Turn meat occasionally and baste with marinade. Bake at 350 degrees. For rare, cook for 20 minutes per pound (140 degrees on meat thermometer); medium, 22 minutes per pound (150 degrees); well done, 25 minutes per pound (170 degrees). If desired, meat may be cooked on a barbecue grill or over coals, following instructions of manufacturer.

COUNTRY-STYLE LAMB

2 pounds lamb, cut into cubes
¾ cup oil
6 tablespoons soy sauce
2 tablespoons Worcestershire sauce
3 tablespoons orange juice
1 tablespoon dry mustard

1 teaspoon coarsely ground black
  pepper
1 teaspoon salt
1 tablespoon chopped fresh parsley
1 clove garlic, minced
Vegetables for skewers (optional)

Place lamb in a large glass container. In a bowl, combine oil, soy sauce, Worcestershire sauce, orange juice, dry mustard, pepper, salt, parsley, and garlic. Mix well. Pour over cubed lamb, and cover container. Refrigerate for up to 24 hours. Remove lamb from marinade and thread pieces on skewers. If desired, alternate lamb cubes with vegetables, such as mushrooms, cherry tomatoes, and chunks of onion or green pepper. Cook on grill, brushing occasionally with marinade. Makes 6 to 8 servings.

BEEF STEAK TERIYAKI

2 pounds sirloin steak, cut into thick
  cubes
⅓ cup chopped onion
2 cloves garlic, minced
1 teaspoon ground ginger

1½ cups soy sauce
¼ cup pineapple juice
⅓ cup molasses
Vegetables for skewers

In a large bowl combine onion, garlic, ginger, soy sauce, pineapple juice, and molasses. Mix well. Add steak cubes. Cover and marinate in refrigerator for 8 hours. Remove meat from marinade and thread on skewers alternately with garden vegetables, such as zucchini, pieces of onion or green pepper, or cherry tomatoes. Cook on grill, basting occasionally with marinade, to desired doneness. Makes 6 to 8 servings.

COWBELLES' MUSHROOM-SAUCED STEAKS

4 beef cube steaks
3 tablespoons flour
Salt to taste
¼ teaspoon pepper
3 tablespoons butter or margarine

1 small onion, chopped
1 cup fresh mushrooms, sliced
½ cup apple juice
½ cup beef broth

Combine flour, salt, and pepper, and dredge cube steaks. In a heavy skillet, heat 2 tablespoons butter, and brown steaks to desired doneness (3 to 4 minutes on each side). Set aside. In a separate skillet, sauté onion in 1 tablespoon butter until tender. Add mushrooms and cook over medium heat 5 minutes, stirring occasionally. Add apple juice and beef broth. Stir over high heat until liquid is reduced by half. Pour mushroom sauce over steaks and simmer until sauce is slightly thickened, about 3 to 4 minutes. Makes 4 servings.

LAVIRD'S VENISON PIQUANT

2 pounds venison
Salt and pepper to taste
¾ cup flour
½ cup butter or cooking oil
¼ teaspoon caraway seeds

1 onion, finely chopped
Juice of ½ lemon
2 cups sour cream
2 beef bouillon cubes, crushed
Steamed white or wild rice

Remove all fat from meat and cut into 2-inch cubes. Season meat with salt and pepper and dredge with flour. In a heavy skillet over medium heat, brown meat in butter or oil. Add caraway seeds, onion, lemon juice, sour cream, and crushed bouillon cubes. Cover and simmer slowly for 1½ to 2 hours. Serve over steamed white or wild rice. Makes 6 servings.

SWEDISH MEAT-FILLED DUMPLINGS

¾ cup mashed potatoes
4½ cups flour
3 eggs, beaten
1 tablespoon salt
1 tablespoon lard or shortening
1 cup plus 2 tablespoons milk

¾ pound ground ham
2 medium onions, chopped
Dash of allspice
Salt and pepper to taste
6 to 8 quarts water

In a large bowl, combine mashed potatoes, flour, beaten eggs, salt, lard or shortening, and milk. Mix to make a soft dough. On floured board, roll dough out ½–inch thick and cut with round cookie cutter. In a separate bowl combine ground ham, onions, allspice, and salt and pepper. Mix well. Put a spoonful of ham mixture on top of each round of dough. Gather the edges of the dough up around the filling in loose, natural folds. Bring the folds up to the top of the ball and twist them securely together. In an 8–quart stockpot, bring water to boil. Drop in dumplings and cover pan. Boil for 30 to 40 minutes. Remove dumplings from pot with a large slotted spoon or strainer. Makes 8 to 10 servings.

SAUSAGE-STUFFED POTATOES

4 large baking potatoes
½ pound ground pork sausage
⅓ cup cream

Salt and pepper to taste
1 cup grated cheddar cheese

Wash and oil skins of potatoes. Bake at 375 degrees for 1½ hours or until done. Remove from oven; cool slightly. Cut potatoes in half. Scoop out potatoes (do not break skins) into a large bowl, and place shells on a baking sheet. Set aside. In a skillet, cook sausage until brown. Drain excess fat. Mash potatoes, then beat in cream, salt, and pepper until fluffy. Stir in sausage and ½ cup of grated cheese. Pile potato mixture into shells. Sprinkle with remaining cheese. Heat at 375 degrees for 10 minutes. Makes 8 servings.

STEAK AND VEGETABLE SOUP

1 can (14 ounces) beef broth
1½ cups water
1 large onion, chopped
2 cups cubed potatoes
1 cup chopped carrots
1 cup frozen peas
1 pound boneless beef top sirloin
   steak, cut in ½–inch pieces

2 teaspoons vegetable oil
1 tablespoon fresh parsley
1 tablespoon fresh chives
1½ teaspoons fresh basil
1 teaspoon fresh thyme
2 tablespoons balsamic vinegar
Salt and pepper to taste

In a large saucepan, combine beef broth, water, onion, potatoes, carrots, and peas. Bring to a boil, then reduce heat and simmer, uncovered, until vegetables are tender, about 15 minutes.

While vegetables are cooking, prepare meat: In a heavy skillet over medium heat, brown steak cubes in oil for 2 to 3 minutes. Add to vegetables, and stir in parsley, chives, basil, thyme, vinegar, salt, and pepper. Heat, then serve. Makes 4 to 6 servings.

SCALLOPED CABBAGE

1 small head cabbage
½ cup evaporated milk or light
   cream

1 cup grated cheddar cheese
Salt and pepper to taste
Buttered bread crumbs

Cut cabbage into chunks. Steam until tender-crisp in a saucepan with a steam insert or in a small amount of water. Drain and set aside. In a saucepan, combine evaporated milk or light cream, grated cheese, salt, and pepper. Over medium heat, stir until cheese is melted and sauce is smooth. Combine sauce and cabbage. Place in a 2–quart casserole dish and sprinkle generously with buttered bread crumbs. Bake at 350 degrees for 30 minutes. Serve hot. Makes 4 to 6 servings.

Contributor's comment: "Many people in our area grow cabbage, and we are always looking for new ways to prepare it. This is one of our favorite dishes."

MEADOW POTATO SOUP

6 slices bacon, cut in small pieces	2 tablespoons butter or margarine
6 medium potatoes, cut in cubes	1 tablespoon flour
1 medium onion, chopped	Salt and pepper to taste
4 cups milk	Water

In a small skillet, fry bacon pieces. In a medium-sized soup kettle, combine bacon, potatoes, and onion; add just enough water to cover. Bring to a boil and simmer until potatoes are tender. In a separate, larger kettle, combine butter or margarine and flour. Add milk and stir until smooth. Add all ingredients from the first kettle, including water. Add salt and pepper to taste. Simmer, covered, 15 to 20 minutes, stirring occasionally. Makes 6 to 8 servings.

SANPETE CARROTS

6 medium or large carrots	3 tablespoons honey
2 tablespoons butter	1 tablespoon fresh parsley

Wash and peel carrots; cut into bite-size pieces. Steam in a saucepan with a steamer or in a small amount of water. Drain. In a small pan, melt butter, then stir in honey and parsley. Pour over carrots. Serve hot. Carrots may also be cooked over hot coals. Wrap well in 2 layers of aluminum foil and bake until tender, about 45 minutes. Makes 4 servings.

Contributor's comment: "Sanpete County is famous for its carrots. In years past, we were fondly known as the 'Carrot County' and our citizens were called 'Carrot Eaters.'"

FRIED GREEN TOMATOES

4 large green tomatoes
2 eggs, beaten
1 can (12 ounces) evaporated milk
⅓ cup water

Salt and pepper to taste
¾ cup flour
¾ cup cornmeal
¼ cup vegetable oil

Wash but do not peel tomatoes. Cut in ¼-inch slices. In a bowl combine eggs, evaporated milk, water, salt, and pepper. Mix flour and cornmeal in a shallow bowl. Dip tomato slices in flour mixture, then egg mixture, then flour again. Heat oil in a skillet. Place floured tomato slices in skillet and fry over medium heat until browned on both sides. Serve hot. Makes 6 to 8 servings.

FRESH CORN SALAD

4 cups fresh corn, cooked and cut
    from cob
½ cup finely chopped green onions
½ cup finely chopped red bell
    pepper
½ cup finely chopped green bell
    pepper
1 clove garlic, crushed

2 ribs celery, chopped
½ cup white wine vinegar
½ cup vegetable oil
¼ cup sugar
Salt and pepper to taste
½ cup diced bacon, fried and
    drained
Leaves of red-leaf lettuce

In a large bowl combine corn, green onions, red pepper, garlic, and celery. In a separate bowl combine vinegar, oil, sugar, salt, and pepper. Pour over corn mixture; mix well. Chill for 8 hours. Add bacon and serve on lettuce leaves. Makes 6 servings.

PIONEER THRUMPITY (WHOLE WHEAT CEREAL)

1 cup whole wheat
3 cups water

Salt to taste

In a saucepan soak wheat in cold water for 12 hours. Add salt and bring to a boil. Add more water if needed. Stirring constantly, simmer until wheat is soft. Serve with honey, molasses, or sugar. Makes 6 to 8 servings.

APPLE BROWN BETTY

4 cups apples, peeled and sliced
½ cup sugar
½ cup water
3 tablespoons lemon juice
½ teaspoon grated lemon rind
¼ teaspoon cinnamon

¼ teaspoon nutmeg
4 cups soft bread crumbs
½ cup butter or margarine, melted
Sweetened whipped cream
  (optional)

In a bowl, combine apple slices, sugar, water, lemon juice, lemon rind, cinnamon, and nutmeg. Stir. Add bread crumbs and melted butter or margarine. Mix well. Place in a buttered 9 x 13–inch pan. Cover and bake at 350 degrees for 40 minutes or until apples are tender. Serve warm with sweetened whipped cream, if desired. Makes 6 servings.

CARROT PUDDING

1 cup grated carrots   1 teaspoon salt
1 cup grated potatoes   1 teaspoon nutmeg
½ cup lard or butter, melted   1 teaspoon ground cloves
1 cup sugar   1 teaspoon allspice
1 cup flour   1 teaspoon baking soda
1 teaspoon cinnamon   Vanilla Sauce (recipe below)

Mix all ingredients together. Spoon into greased tin cans or pudding molds, filling only one-half full (pudding expands as it cooks). Cover each tin tightly with lid, aluminum foil, or several layers of cheesecloth secured by rubber band. Place a rack or inverted heavy saucer in bottom of heavy saucepan or Dutch oven. Add water to depth of 2 inches; bring to boil. Place tightly covered tins of pudding on rack. Cover and boil gently for 2½ hours. Serve warm with Vanilla Sauce. Serves 6 to 8.

VANILLA SAUCE

½ cup butter   ½ cup heavy cream
1 cup sugar   1 teaspoon vanilla

In saucepan or top of double boiler placed over boiling water, combine butter, sugar, and cream. Stirring occasionally, cook until smooth. Remove from heat, and stir in vanilla. Serve warm sauce over Carrot Pudding or other steamed pudding.

Note: Sauce becomes solidified when it is cooled. To serve, reheat and, if necessary, add a little cream or milk.

Contributor's comment: "This recipe is from my grandmother, who is ninety-five years old. She got it from her mother."

MANTI WHOLE WHEAT BREAD

1 package (1 tablespoon) active dry
    yeast
4¼ cups warm water (divided)
3 tablespoons honey or molasses
½ cup shortening, melted

2½ teaspoons salt
6 cups whole wheat flour
2 cups white flour
½ cup powdered milk

Dissolve yeast in ¼ cup warm water; set aside. In a large bowl, combine 4 cups warm water, honey, shortening, and salt. Add whole wheat flour, white flour, and powdered milk. Mix well for 10 minutes. Divide dough in half and put into 2 well-greased 9 x 5 x 3-inch loaf pans. Cover lightly with a clean dish towel, and let rise in a warm place until double in bulk, about 30 minutes. Bake at 375 degrees for 30 minutes.

SCANDINAVIAN WHEAT BREAD

1 medium potato
3 cups water
1 package (1 tablespoon) active dry
    yeast
¼ cup lukewarm water

2 tablespoons honey
2 teaspoons salt
2 tablespoons oil
3 cups whole wheat flour
3 cups white flour

Wash, peel, and dice one medium potato. Place in a saucepan with 3 cups water. Simmer until tender. Drain, saving 2 cups of the potato water. Mash potato. Dissolve yeast in ¼ cup lukewarm water. In a large bowl, combine potato water, yeast, mashed potato, honey, salt, oil, and 2 cups whole wheat flour. Beat together for five minutes. Continue adding wheat and white flours until dough can be kneaded into a smooth ball. Cover and let rise until double in bulk. Punch down and knead again for 5 to 10 minutes. Cover and let rise again. Divide dough in half, and shape into 2 loaves. Place in greased 9 x 5 x 3-inch loaf pans. Cover lightly with clean dish towel and let rise 20 to 30 minutes. Bake at 375 degrees for 30 minutes.

GLAZED DOUGHNUTS OR CINNAMON ROLLS

2 cups milk
7 tablespoons shortening
2 packages (2 tablespoons) active
   dry yeast
½ cup warm water
1 cup mashed potatoes
3 eggs

½ teaspoon vanilla
½ teaspoon lemon extract
1 teaspoon salt
½ cup sugar
6 to 7 cups flour
Oil for deep-frying
Glaze (recipe on page 195)

In a saucepan over medium heat, scald milk. Remove from heat and add shortening; stir until shortening melts. Set aside to cool. Dissolve yeast in ½ cup warm water. Set aside. Pour milk and shortening mixture into a large bowl. Stir in mashed potatoes, eggs, yeast, vanilla, lemon extract, salt, and sugar. Mix well. Add flour to form soft dough; knead until smooth and elastic. Cover and let rise in a warm place until 2½ times in bulk. Punch down. Cover and let rise 15 minutes or until double in bulk.

To make doughnuts: On a floured board, roll out dough. Cut with floured doughnut cutter. Cover and let rise until double in size. Fry in hot oil, turning once. Sprinkle with sugar or dip in glaze. Makes about 3 dozen doughnuts.

To make cinnamon rolls: After dough has risen twice, roll on a floured board into a 12 x 16-inch rectangle about ½ inch thick. Spread favorite filling over rectangle to about 1 inch from edge, or spread with melted butter; sprinkle with cinnamon and sugar and, if desired, raisins. Gently roll up dough from long side. Cut with sharp scissors or knife into slices 1¼ to 1½ inch thick. Place on greased cookie sheet, with rolls not touching. Cover loosely and let rise until double in size. Bake at 350 degrees for 20 minutes. Frost while warm with a confectioners' sugar icing (confectioners' sugar mixed with small amount of hot water), if desired. Makes 2½ to 3 dozen cinnamon rolls.

GLAZE FOR DOUGHNUTS

3 cups confectioners' sugar
½ teaspoon cream of tartar
½ teaspoon vanilla

Dash of salt
⅓ cup hot water (approximately)

Mix together confectioners' sugar, cream of tartar, vanilla, and salt, adding enough hot water to make glaze the consistency of a medium syrup.

Contributor's comment: "Making these doughnuts each year during the deer hunt is a tradition in our area. Many are sold to hungry deer hunters, but most are eaten by deer hunters' wives and children left at home."

BAKED APPLE CRISP

4 cups sliced apples
1½ cups water
⅓ cup granulated sugar
1 tablespoon lemon juice
¼ teaspoon nutmeg
⅛ teaspoon salt
½ cup butter or margarine

½ cup flour
½ teaspoon salt
½ cup brown sugar
½ cup granulated sugar
⅓ cup grated cheddar cheese
Sweetened whipped cream

In a heavy saucepan, combine apples, water, ⅓ cup granulated sugar, lemon juice, and nutmeg. Stir over medium heat until mixture boils and thickens. Pour apples into a 9–inch greased baking dish. In a separate bowl, combine butter or margarine, flour, salt, brown sugar, and ½ cup granulated sugar. Mix to a crumble texture. Put crumble over apples, and sprinkle with grated cheese. Bake at 350 degrees for 25 to 30 minutes, or until golden brown. Serve warm with sweetened whipped cream. Makes 6 to 8 servings.

CARROT CAKE

2 cups sugar
1¼ cups oil
4 eggs
3 cups grated carrots
2½ cups flour

1 teaspoon salt
2 teaspoons baking soda
2 teaspoons cinnamon
Cream Cheese Frosting (recipe below)

In a large mixing bowl, cream sugar, oil, and eggs. Add carrots and mix well. Stir or sift together flour, salt, baking soda, and cinnamon. Stir into carrot mixture. Mix well. Pour batter into a greased and floured 9 x 13–inch baking pan. Bake at 350 degrees for 30 minutes. Cool, then frost with Cream Cheese Frosting.

CREAM CHEESE FROSTING

½ cup butter or margarine
1 small package (3 ounces) cream cheese

1 teaspoon vanilla
2½ cups confectioners' sugar

In a mixing bowl combine butter or margarine, cream cheese, and vanilla. Stir in confectioners' sugar, and beat until smooth. Spread on cooled cake.

SOUR CREAM MAPLE NUT CAKE

2 cups heavy cream
½ teaspoon white vinegar
3 eggs
1⅓ cups sugar
1 teaspoon maple flavoring
2⅓ cups flour

2 teaspoons baking powder
1 teaspoon baking soda
½ teaspoon salt
½ cup chopped walnuts
Caramel Frosting (recipe on page 127)

Stir vinegar into heavy cream. Set aside. In a large mixing bowl beat eggs. Add cream, sugar, and maple flavoring. Beat well. Stir or sift together flour, baking powder, baking soda, and salt. Add to egg mixture; mix well. Stir in nuts. Pour batter into a greased and floured 13 x 9–inch baking pan. Bake at 375 degrees for 35 minutes. Cool, then frost with Caramel Frosting.

OLD-TIME CINNAMON JUMBLES

¾ cup sugar
3 teaspoons cinnamon
1½ cups shortening or butter
3 cups sugar
3 eggs

2½ cups buttermilk
3 teaspoons vanilla
6 cups flour
1½ teaspoons baking soda
1½ teaspoons salt

Mix together ¾ cup sugar and the cinnamon; set aside. In a bowl, cream together shortening or butter, 3 cups sugar, and eggs. Stir in buttermilk and vanilla. Sift together flour, baking soda, and salt. Stir into creamed mixture; mix well. Chill dough until it thickens. Drop rounded teaspoonfuls about 2 inches apart on lightly greased baking sheet. Sprinkle generously with sugar-cinnamon mixture. Bake at 400 degrees until lightly browned, about 8 to 10 minutes. Makes approximately 5 dozen cookies.

MOM'S APPLE DUMPLINGS

2 cups flour
2 teaspoons baking powder
1 teaspoon salt
¾ cup lard or shortening
½ cup cold milk
6 baking apples, peeled and chopped
2 teaspoons cinnamon

1 cup sugar
½ cup chopped walnuts or pecans
Apple Dumpling Sauce (recipe
  below)
Sweetened whipped cream or vanilla
  ice cream (optional)

Combine flour, baking powder, and salt. Cut in shortening until mixture resembles small peas. Stir in milk and mix together. Place dough on floured board and knead 6 to 8 times. Roll into rectangle about 12 x 16 inches in size.

In a bowl, combine apples, cinnamon, sugar, and nuts. Spread on the dough to about 1 inch from edges. Gently roll up dough from long side. With scissors or sharp knife, cut in 1½-inch slices, as for cinnamon rolls. Put into a greased 9 x 13-inch baking dish.

Prepare sauce (recipe below). Pour over dumplings and bake at 350 degrees for 35 minutes, or until rolls are golden brown. Serve warm with warm sauce and, if desired, sweetened whipped cream or vanilla ice cream. Makes 1 dozen dumplings.

APPLE DUMPLING SAUCE

2 cups brown sugar
2 cups hot water
⅓ cup butter

¼ teaspoon cinnamon
1 teaspoon vanilla

In a 3-quart saucepan, combine ingredients. Stirring constantly, cook over medium heat until sugar is dissolved. Serve warm.

Comment from contributor in Mount Pleasant: "Nearly everyone in our area has an apple tree. This recipe is at least 150 years old."

ANGEL FOOD PIE

1 baked 9-inch pie shell
4½ tablespoons cornstarch
¾ cup sugar
1½ cups boiling water
½ teaspoon salt
3 egg whites, at room temperature

3 tablespoons sugar
1½ teaspoons vanilla
Caramel Sauce (recipe below)
Peanut brittle, crushed
Sweetened whipped cream

Prepare pie shell, using favorite recipe. Set aside. In saucepan, mix cornstarch and ¾ cup sugar. Add boiling water. Cook, stirring constantly, until clear, about 10 to 12 minutes. Remove from heat. In a mixing bowl, add salt to egg whites; beat until stiff. Add 3 tablespoons of sugar and vanilla. Continue beating until egg whites are creamy. Pour the hot cornstarch mixture over egg whites slowly, beating constantly. Cool slightly. Pour into pastry shell and chill for at least 2 hours. To serve, cut in individual serving pieces, then pour a thin layer of caramel sauce over each piece. Top with crushed peanut brittle and a dollop of sweetened whipped cream. Makes 6 to 8 servings.

CARAMEL SAUCE

2 tablespoons butter
1¼ cups brown sugar
2 tablespoons dark corn syrup

½ cup light cream
½ teaspoon vanilla

In a saucepan over medium heat, melt butter. Add brown sugar, corn syrup, and cream. Simmer, stirring constantly, until sugar is dissolved, about 1 minute. Simmer until sauce reaches desired syrup consistency. Remove from heat and add vanilla. (If sauce becomes too thick, dilute with a little cream or milk.)

IDA DELIGHT'S LEMON PIE

1 baked 9-inch pie shell
2 egg yolks
2 cups water
1 cup sugar

½ teaspoon salt
4 tablespoons cornstarch
¼ cup fresh lemon juice
1 heaping tablespoon butter

Prepare and bake pie shell, using favorite recipe. Beat egg yolks; set aside. In a large saucepan, bring water to boil. Mix sugar, salt, and cornstarch, and add to boiling water. Return to boiling and let boil until clear, stirring constantly. Stir a small amount of hot mixture into beaten egg yolks; then, stirring constantly, add yolks to boiling mixture. Add lemon juice and butter. Remove from heat and let cool slightly. Pour into baked pie shell and top with meringue or whipped cream. Makes 6 to 8 servings.

Comment from eighty-seven-year-old contributor: "This was my mother's recipe for lemon pie as long ago as I can remember."

HONEY CANDY

½ cup water
1 cup honey

1 cup sugar
¼ teaspoon baking soda

Butter a baking sheet. Set aside. In a saucepan, combine water, honey, and sugar. Boil, stirring occasionally, until candy reaches hard-ball stage (about 260 degrees on candy thermometer). Remove from heat and add baking soda. Pour into buttered pans. Cool. Break into bite-size pieces. Makes 1 pound.

ACKNOWLEDGMENTS

I wish to extend my heartfelt thanks to Julie M. Shipman for her generous contribution to this publication. As author of the introduction and histories of the nine travel regions, Julie has been instrumental in bringing this work to fruition. This book has been positively influenced by her distinctive talents and the many tireless hours of unselfish support.

—Paula Julander

I would like to acknowledge and extend my personal thanks to the many people who have contributed to the success of this book. I am grateful for the inspiration for the book that I received while traveling throughout this beautiful state of Utah and meeting its wonderful people. I also want to express my heartfelt love and gratitude to my family and friends for their support and encouragement—most especially my dear mother, who taught me the traditional joys of cooking and sharing, and my supportive father and family members, who willingly sampled many cooking creations.

—Joanne Milner

We wish to extend our thanks to the publishing staff at Deseret Book Company: editors Eleanor Knowles and Emily Watts, designer Shauna Gibby, and typographer Tonya Facemyer. Thanks also to Russell Winegar for the photography, and Kathryn Trulson, who helped prepare the food for the photographs. And we especially thank the many people throughout the state of Utah who sent us their family recipes, stories, and traditions. Without them, this book would not have been possible. Their names are listed below:

Alexgard, Kathy
Allen, Karla
Allen, Deborah
Andersen, Tammy
    and Brad

Andrews, Liz
Barnes, Roger
Beattie, Joy
Beckstrom, Barbara
Benik, Mary K. Bettes

Best, Connie
Bikakis, Terry
Black, Mary
Brotherson, Shauna W.
Bytheway, Frieda

Cardon, Kathleen
Chappell, Linda
Clayson, Beulah M.
Cowley, Camille
Danies, Jean
Davis, Julie
DeJournette, Daun
    and Dick
Dennis, June
Desmond, June
Deuel, Ann and Kerry
Dunham, Nancy
    and Gene
Evans, Dean
Fawcett, Arvilla R.
Frisby, Kathy
Garr, Helen
Glendale Town Board
Goode, Elizabeth
Hansen, Colleen
Hansen, LaVird
Hayes, Mary Lois
Hayes, Fred M.
Higley, Armeta Stoker
Horrocks, Garth and Joy
Humphrey, Merene
    and Tom
Humphrey, Mark
Humphreys, Dale
Hunsaker, Fred R.
Hunt, Augusta W.

Jensen, Jamie
Jones, Alice
Julander, Paula F.
Kenyon-Bares, Helen
Kraync, Karl
Kukendall, Emma R.
Larsson, Mitch
Leavitt, Jacalyn
Lund, Gwen
Lyman Town
McAllister, Joan S.
McQuarrie, Howard
Mendel, Anna
Milius, Sheran K.
Milner, Giovanna F.
Milner, Joanne R.
Morgan, Edna
Morgan, Betty
Moroni City Corporation
Nagel, Sophie
Nielson, Bryce
Nielson, Bob and Lowella
O'Brien, Ann
Olsen, Dorothy
Ovard, Reta F.
Page, Mary Ann
Palmer, Dorothy
Pinder, Phebe
Plymouth City
Pope, Connie
Price, Clara and Dan

Price, Mattie
Proctor, Lucile H.
Proctor, Debra
Robertson, Vangie
Rosenvall, Vernice
Rowley, Shirley
Russell, Emma
Sampinos, Nick
Saunders, Kristine S.
Schaefermeyer, Shanna
Sherry, Lee
Shill, Fern G.
Sorensen, Susan
Spendlove, Deyon E.
Steele, Lucile
Stewart, Arden
Taylor, Diane
Topolovec, Rosemary
USU Extension Service,
    Davis County
Utah Cattlemen and Wool
    Growers Association
Veibell, Jeanne and Floyd
Ward, Vernice
Wells, Annette
Whitington, Virginia
Wiberg, Beverly
Winward, Alta
Yardley, Kathy

INDEX